J.N. Macleod, Christmas 1973, Scrabster

£2.50

WHISKY

Frontispiece: Discussion about the recent increase in the price of whisky on Leith Pier. Edinburgh Broadsheet 1742.

Whisky

James Ross

LONDON
ROUTLEDGE & KEGAN PAUL

First published 1970
by Routledge & Kegan Paul Ltd
Broadway House, 68–74 Carter Lane
London E.C.4
Printed in Great Britain
by Western Printing Services Ltd, Bristol
© James Ross 1970
ISBN 0 7100 6685 6

Contents

	List of Illustrations	vii
	Preface	ix
	Acknowledgements	xi
1	HOW IT BEGAN	1
2	SCOTSMAN AND ENGLISHMAN: MALT AND GIN	8
3	CONVIVIAL SOCIETY	21
4	BAD LAWS AND THE ILLICIT STILL	58
5	MOONLIGHT INTO DAYLIGHT	88
6	PROOF	94
7	THE MAKING OF WHISKY	100
8	WHISKY, WHISKEY AND USQUEBAUGH	116
9	EXPANSION: THE 'WHAT IS WHISKY?' CASE	123
10	THE INDUSTRY OF TODAY	144
	Further Reading	153
	Index	155

List of Illustrations

Frontispiece. Discussion about the recent increase in the price of whisky on Leith Pier. In *Edinburgh Broadsheet*, 1742

between pages 26 and 27

1 Rory Mor Macleod's drinking horn and cup, Dunvegan Castle, against the background of the Fairy flag
2 Three men from Islay. Whisky at the centre of folktale collecting
3 The De'il's awa' wi' th' Exciseman. From an etching by Bryden
4 Auld Gudeman ye're a Drucken Carle. From an etching by Walter Geikie

between pages 42 and 43

5 Amen Glass, eighteenth century
6 Jacobite Glass, with coloured likeness of the Young Pretender
7 Burns's reply to James Steuart
8 Gill and Mutchkin measures, seventeenth century

between pages 122 and 123

9 The Scots Pint or Tappit Hen
10 Highland bothy – the alarm. An early posed photograph
11 Poteen making in Connemara. Children watching the still
12 Whisky on its way in 1924
13 Irish pot still containing 18,000 gallons
14 Highland pot stills. 'A multiplicity of small stills'

vii

Preface

The precise history of Scotch whisky in its earliest phase is difficult to write. Its evolution becomes clear only when controls are slapped on it and governments make edicts seeking to gain from it. A detailed history would therefore be very much a matter of a study of restrictive legislation.

The story of whisky is one of adversity, a slow birth from the confines of monasteries and the controls of Barber Surgeons and the like, to a rough adolescence passed in conflict with the law. In the Highlands in the late eighteenth century, after the Highlander had his weapons, his tartan and his clan torn from him and when there seemed to be no cause left to fight for, another cause appeared in the restrictive legislation about whisky. In his struggle to preserve his traditional drink, it seemed that another heroic age was beginning. When the Gaelic poet sang:

> *Tha bainne aig na caoraich uile*
> *'S tha galan aig a' chaora chruim*
>
> While all the ewes have milk
> My crooked-horned ewe has a gallon . . .

he was celebrating his victory over the roving Exciseman. The 'ewe with the crooked horn' or 'the one-horned and one-eared cow' was the Exciseman's target. The portable illicit still and its all-important worm kept the good name of Scotch whisky alive in an age of harsh legislation. Although pious men repeatedly abhorred these breaches of the law, a grateful public did not regard their activities as criminal, and with sober hindsight, neither need we. The small illicit distillers in the Highland

ix

glens, and indeed in more exotic places such as the crypts of Lowland churches and the hollow arches of city bridges, kept the traditional skills of pot distilling alive until it was possible to apply these skills openly once more.

The owners of the great blends of today, household names though they be, would admit immediately the existence of the 'imponderables' of distilling. The Highland distiller of today is the apprentice of his master, and the basis of his knowledge lies in the absorption of generations of traditional knowledge.

While the dominant position of Scotch whisky in the world today is based primarily on the pot, or malt, distiller, another great phase in its development came with people of commercial genius who saw the possibility of its greatness and worked to bring it to such a position. The poet who sang

> My ewie wi' the crooked horn
> Weel deserved baith gerse and corn;
> Sic a ewe was never born
> Hereabout or far awa'

could never have conceived that his little 'ewie' could grow into the great many-headed mammoth that it is today.

In this book we shall look at the beginnings of Scotch whisky, its history, its lore, and at least some of the varied processes that have combined to make it what it is.

Acknowledgements

I am deeply indebted to numerous people in the distilling profession, both in Scotland and in Ireland. Without them any description of the production of whisky would have been impossible. They gave valuable information with patience and courtesy. My sincere thanks also to the Edinburgh Public Library, the National Museum of Antiquities of Scotland, and to Ralph Morton of the School of Scottish Studies of Edinburgh University.

TO WHISKY

Is coisiche na h-oidhche thu
Gu leapannan na maighdeannan;
A Righ! gur h-iomadh loinn a th'ort
Gu coibhneas thoirt a gruagach.

You are the prowler of the night
To the beds of virgins;
O God! what powers you have
To gain kindness from girls.

A Gaelic Toast

1

How it Began

Let us begin with a definition of alcohol itself. According to Chambers' *Encyclopedia*, the process of distilling is, in fact, 'that of separating the different elements in a liquor by volatilization and condensation', i.e. vaporizing a liquid and then recovering what remains of it by condensing it. The formation of clouds and the fall of rain is a natural example. A. Cooper in *The Complete Distiller*, published in London in 1803, describes the process more poetically: 'Distillation is the art of separating, or drawing off, the spirituous, aqueous and oleaginous parts of a mixed body from the grosser, and more terrestrial parts, by means of fire, and condensing them again by cold.'

The art of distillation is by no means a modern piece of knowledge. In his *Meteorology* written in the fourth century before Christ, Aristotle observes that sea-water can be made drinkable by distillation, and that wine and other liquids can be submitted to the same process. In the Middle Ages, however, the purpose of distillation was not to satisfy mere thirst or the urge for jollification. To the chemists, or, as we should say, the alchemists of that period, it was a divine process which they manipulated in their search for the panacea. Indeed, the thirteenth-century physician, Arnold de Villa Nova, thought that he had found the universal cure for all evils and disorders when he found a distillation of wine. An alchemist from Majorca, Raymond Lully, writing in the same century, saw alcohol in a similar light. He claimed it to be 'an emanation of divinity' and thought of it as an element 'newly revealed to man, but hid from antiquity, because the human race was then too young to need this beverage designed to revive the energies of modern decrepitude'. His description of distilling is relevant to us today: 'the true water of life will come over in precious drops, which, being rectified by two or three successive distillations, will afford the wonderful quintessence of wine'.

It is difficult to fix anything like a firm date to the beginning of whisky distilling in these islands. The words 'aqua vitae', 'the water of life', are ambiguous. Certainly in the Middle Ages in temperate Europe it meant the spirit of distilled wine – brandy, and this name came to be applied also to the spirit distilled from malted barley. Undoubtedly, distilling of the latter kind went on while brandy was being imported, and perhaps even being made from imported or locally grown wines. So the consumption of brandy, and even the making of it, merges with the production of whisky, and when we read in the *Annals of Clonmacnoise* under the year 1405 that 'Richard Magranell, chieftain of Moyntyreolas, died at Christmas by taking a surfeit of aqua vitae', we do not know whether his final drink was malt spirit or brandy.

In Scotland, the first definite evidence that we have of the making of whisky is an entry in the Exchequer Rolls for the year 1494–5. It is quite unequivocal: 'To Friar John Cor, by order of the King, to make aquavitae, VIII bolls of malt.' This is the first of a series of nineteen entries between 1495 and 1512. They occur in the Accounts of the Lord High Treasurer as well as in the Exchequer Rolls. It is interesting that we find them in the latter part of the reign of James IV, King of Scots, a pseudo-scientific experimenter and patron of alchemists. For instance the words 'aqua vitae' occur frequently in connection with the researches of John Damien, Abbot of Tungland, who was a well-known alchemist. Those who are acquainted with the by-ways of Scottish history may have heard of Damien's attempt to fly, equipped with wings of his own making, from the walls of Stirling Castle. King James was among those who witnessed his failure, and heard Damien's explanation that among the feathers on his wings were hen's feathers, and that hens aspired more to the midden than to the heavens. Nevertheless, the king later tried to obtain a pension for him, presumably so that he could continue his scientific experiments.

We have other early evidence of widespread distilling in Scotland, such as that from the Act of 1579. In modernized language, the preamble of this act states:

> Forasmuch as it appears that victuals shall be scarce this present year, and understanding that there is a great quantity of malt consumed in all parts of this realm in the making of aqua vitae, this is one great reason for the dearth within the same. It lays down, therefore, that only Earls, Lords, Barons, and Gentlemen for their own use shall distil any.

This Act makes it appear that the making of whisky was so widespread as to influence the supplies of grain. Further back, the Act of 1555 dealing with trade between the western burghs and the islands, gives the inhabitants of those burghs the right to barter bread, ale and aqua vitae with the islands in exchange for other merchandise.

So it seems that despite the late appearance of the first Act of Excise, whisky was in common use in Scotland during the previous century and a half at least. According to Fynes Morison, the inhabitants of the Western Highlands included aqua vitae among the goods which they traded with Ireland. If they were at all like their descendants we can be sure that they had a good surplus before they exported it. In Edinburgh too in the middle of the century there were a number of convictions relating to breaches of the privileges granted to the city Barber Surgeons.

However meagre an account of the history of whisky that one

may wish to write, it cannot be separable from the progress of the 'gentle pressure of the fiscal hand'. Our sources for the history of spirits lie in legislation about them. In the very first piece of written evidence that we have about the making of whisky quoted above, we have the words 'by order of the King'. In 1506 the same king granted a monopoly in the manufacturing of 'aqua vitae' within the precincts of the City of Edinburgh, to the Guild of Surgeon Barbers. His charter ordered that 'no persons, man nor woman, within this burgh, make nor sell aquavitae except the said Masters, Brethren or Freemen'. It must not be thought that this indicated that the influence of the Church was being weakened by the granting of this sole right in the production of spirits. It is more probably another indication of the strong connection between the Church and the practice of surgery. The rights granted were probably of some value although we have no means as yet of knowing just how much. While the Edinburgh Burgh Council Records of this period contain prices for wine, beer and malt, they do not mention whisky. Perhaps control over the production and sale of it was removed from the city's jurisdiction through this monopoly.

In the early eighteenth century whisky was still not the most popular drink in Scotland. The drink most widely consumed was undoubtedly ale. Its production was not as yet centralized in big breweries and was simply a secondary occupation of the farm population in most parishes. Along with ale, the upper classes added imported beverages from France, Spain and Madeira – claret, brandy, sherry and others. Claret was undoubtedly the most popular of these and was drunk to excess. Drinking tended to go on right round the clock and people would tend to think that they were lacking in hospitality if they did not make their guests drunk. Simon Fraser's entertainment at Castle Downie was famous, as was that of his protagonist and neighbour Forbes, at Culloden House. In both establishments, stretcher-bearers stood by to carry the faint off to their bedrooms. Every place at Simon's table would be full. At the top end with him, above the salt, would be his personal guests and nearest relatives. Further down, below the salt, would be poor or junior relatives or even humble retainers. Food and drink was dispensed to each according to his station – from claret and champagne at the top to whisky-punch and beer at the bottom.

As the eighteenth century progressed, the habitual morning refreshment of a draught of spirits or strong ale was giving way gradually to tea and coffee. Writing of the 1730s, Macintosh of Borlum said:

> When I came to a friend's house in the morning I used to be asked if I had my morning draught yet. I am now asked if I have yet had my tea. And in lieu of the big Quaigh with strong ale and toast, and after a dram of good wholesome Scots spirits, there is now the tea kettle put to the fire, the tea table and silver and china equipage brought in, with marmalet, cream and cold tea.

Although whisky was challenged by other beverages, it still retained a particular kind of prestige. In the Highlands particularly, it was widely used and thought to have a special food value and important medicinal properties. For instance, a traveller in 1736 said: 'The ruddy complexion, nimbleness of these people is not owing to the water drinking but to the aqua vitae, a malt spirit which is commonly used both as victual and drink.' To a certain extent this is the Highland view to this day.

We must remember, however, that the Highlander was not alone in his view. For instance, the consumption of brandy, the only spirit of which we have a fairly precise record in that year, rose in 1832 from 39,000 gallons to 69,000 gallons. This was the year of the great cholera epidemic which began at Sunderland and proceeded to Edinburgh, Glasgow, and to other towns in Lowland Scotland, and alcoholic spirits were supposed to be an efficient antidote to it. This was not simply the view of the ordinary man in the street. Responsible medical opinion throughout Britain held such a view as well, and it was not until comparatively recent times that a different view was adopted.

It might be a digression, but an interesting one, to remember the case of Robert Warner, a total abstainer. In the year 1840, he applied to a life insurance company in London for a policy on his life. He was told that being a total abstainer, he would have to pay an extra premium. The company were being guided by medical advice and their doctors believed that the lives of abstainers were shorter than those of regular drinkers. This applicant thought this untrue and he personally founded a Provident Institution for total abstainers. It was not until 1871 that a number of the leading medical men in England signed a medical declaration which called attention to 'the inconsiderate prescription of alcoholic liquids by medical men' and urged that 'alcohol in any form should be prescribed with as much care as any powerful drug'. This view came to be accepted slowly by the general run of medical practitioners.

Let us return to the early history of the making of whisky in Scotland. Any precise information is scant. We know that it was not until 1644 that the Scots Parliament passed an Act of Excise. This first Excise Act came at a time when public money was badly needed in Scotland. According to the Solemn League and Covenant signed in September 1643, Scotland undertook to send an army into England to help the English Parliament in its war against Charles I. The English Parliament had agreed to contribute £31,000 sterling towards the upkeep of the army of 21,000 men that was raised, but that was not enough. Although the 1644 Act did not establish machinery for the collecting of duties, and although the gentlemen later known as 'gaugers' had not yet made their appearance, we must regard this date as the year of birth of smuggling. This was when smuggling, in the sense of cheating the Revenue, began. There had been breaches of monopoly before and these had been punished, but

6

the Act of 1644 provided the public with the first incentive to cross swords with the ruling of Parliament. England just beat the Scots to it in their imposition of Excise duties. Their first Ordinance in this respect was laid down on 8 September 1643, to be in effect for one year only:

> For all strong waters and aqua vitae, imported or to be imported, to be paid by the first buyer thereof from the merchant or importer and so after that rate for a greater or lesser quantity, after the rate of eightpence per gallon. . . . And for all strong waters and aqua vitae made or distilled within the Realm, Dominion of Wales or Towne of Berwick, the like rate to be paid by the maker or distiller thereof.

The duty fixed by the Act of 1644 was 2s. 8d. Scots per pint for whisky or any other strong liquor. The Scots' pint was about one-third of a gallon. There was a big reduction to 2s. per quart in 1655. Two years later, we see the beginnings of the familiar Excise control of manufacture and the appearance of the 'gaugers', those officers who had the power to 'gauge' or measure containers. In 1661 the direct tax on the home distilled spirit disappeared and a rather obscure kind of malt tax appeared. This was removed in 1695 when the direct tax was once more imposed. As we shall see, this subject of the malt tax was to cause a lot of ill-feeling between Scotland and England in the early decades of the following century.

2

Scotsman and Englishman: Malt and Gin

At the time of the Treaty of Union between Scotland and England in 1707, there was a tax on malt in England but not in Scotland. This was a major point of difference and the Articles of the Union provided that malt should not be taxed in Scotland. One Article also contained the statement that any malt made in Scotland should not be taxed 'during the present war'. In 1713, however, the Treaty of Utrecht brought the 'present war' to an end and the barley growers of England became very resentful of the immunity of the Scots from the tax. Under pressure, the Government in that year extended the tax to Scotland. This move aroused such an uproar, which included a motion in the House of Lords, that it was not enforced. The Scots thought it was a breach of the Union agreement and 'free malt' was a popular slogan of the times. In 1725 the administration of Lord Walpole decided to enforce the tax in Scotland. Although the new tax was only half the English rate, it was seen as an unconstitutional violation of the Treaty. Matters were made much worse by the Government's appointment of English officers of Excise as collectors of the tax. To quote C. de B. Murray in his book on Forbes of Culloden, 'the Scotsman's annoyance at paying twice as much for his claret and his whisky as he had done before the Union was in no way mollified by the discovery that the man who took the money spoke with an English accent and attended the Episcopalian Church'.

The new tax was due to be collected on 23 June, and when the Excise officers entered the city of Glasgow on that day, the maltsters refused them permission to enter their warehouses. Some trouble must have been anticipated because arrangements had already been made for two companies of infantry to be quartered in the town and placed at the disposal of the Provost and magistrates. Riots took place, and the troubles became known as the Malt Tax Riots.

The estimated revenue to be gained by this tax of approximately 3d. per bushel of malt amounted to £20,000 sterling per annum. It would seem to be far too small a sum to justify the ill-feeling which it caused. Perhaps we should see it as one instance of Prime Ministers in London insisting on asserting their authority in the north, even at the expense of infringing the Union agreements. Indeed, it is probable that it was not the effects of the tax, as judged at that time, that sparked off the serious rioting in Glasgow, but the widespread sensitivity about Union breaches. It seems to be fairly clear also that the Provost and the bailies of the city had the power to control the rioting with the military units that had been placed under their orders. Provost Miller's professed fear that a show of violence towards the rioters would only irritate them further, and his concern for the wet clothing of the troops after the long march from Dumbarton, do not seem genuine. In obedience to the Provost's instructions, they were duly billeted in separate quarters. It was at this time, when the soldiers were safely incapacitated, that Daniel Campbell's mansion of Shawfield and its grounds were looted and destroyed. Campbell was Member of Parliament for the Glasgow Burghs and was known to be a supporter of the Government. At 11 p.m. on the 24th, about one hour after the rioters had entered the house, Captain Bushell approached the Provost to say that he was ready to obey his commands to quell the mob. It appears that he was told to keep his soldiers within their quarters.

On the following day, as the town was becoming quieter, the Provost ordered that some of the rioters should be arrested. In

9

light of their victorious rampage of the day before, the citizens felt insulted. Led by a woman beating a drum, large numbers of them attacked the gaol and released the prisoners. Then they attacked the unfortunate soldiers with stones until the patient Captain Bushell had to ask his men to fire. The people then became more angry and seized the town's magazines, arming themselves with such weapons as they could find there. The Provost became thoroughly alarmed and ordered the troops, for the safety and peace of the town, to leave it as quickly as possible. In their retreat to Dumbarton Castle on the afternoon of 25 June, they were pursued by the citizens and some ten or twelve individuals lost their lives.

Because of the apparent neutrality of the Provost and bailies of Glasgow towards riotous assemblies against a government edict, the law began to move against them. The maltsters of Hamilton, Paisley, Ayr and other towns followed the example of Glasgow and shut their doors against the Excise officers and assaulted them. The situation looked serious and would get worse if Glasgow was allowed to escape unpunished. Accordingly the Lord Advocate of Scotland was urged from London to take steps to prosecute the offenders immediately, particularly those who had demolished Shawfield and those guilty of murder. Although they could be tried for High Treason for pursuing the King's troops, it was imperative that they should be dealt with quickly and effectively to discourage unrest elsewhere – Murder, Felony and Riot would be sufficient charges to prefer. The Provost was also to be proceeded against for not reading the Riot Act and the behaviour of the magistrates was to be inquired into. Meanwhile the city had to be thoroughly subdued, and the task fell upon the famous road-maker, General Wade. He was diverted from an expedition to the Highlands and he entered Glasgow on 9 July, bringing with him an imposing force, including Lord Deloraine's Regiment of Foot, six troops of Royal Scots Dragoons, an Independent Company of Lochaber Highlanders and a battery of artillery. On the same day, the long-suffering Captain Bushell returned to the city from Dumbarton. Needless to say, there was immediate peace and the task of detecting the law-breakers began. Three days later, about forty suspects were arrested, including women and children. Little information was discovered from them by questioning, nor from the examination of the magistrates. The excuses tendered by the City Fathers are interesting. Bailie Mitchell, himself a maltster, saw no riotous assemblies whatsoever on the crucial day of 24 June, and the first inkling he had that anything unusual had occurred was when he went to his own malt kiln at 5 o'clock on the following morning and saw the smouldering ruins of Shawfield. At nine on that morning, on the very day that the citizens were drumming the King's soldiers out of town, he left for Port Glasgow to be married. John Stark, the Dean of Guild, did not know that Captain Bushell's troops had been directed to separate billets on the evening of the 22nd, instead of being asked to secure the town's guard room from the mob. He had 'been abroad in the fields taking a walk'. Bailies Stirling and Johnston just knew nothing – they were simply out of town. The Provost blamed the Town Guard of between fifty and sixty burgesses for neglecting their duty. He had ordered the mounting of this guard after the troops had gone to their quarters. As to the charge of failing to read the Riot Act, he claimed that he was dissuaded from doing so by the danger from the mob, and his lack of support.

The result of this inquiry was the arrest and the committal to the Glasgow Tolbooth on 16 July of Provost Miller, the three bailies, Dean of Guild Stark and Deacon Convener John Armour. Bail was refused and on the following day they left for Edinburgh with an armed escort. Bail was finally granted on the 20th and they were released to a great welcome from the Edinburgh crowds. On their arrival in Glasgow, the citizens of that town, of whom the Provost had professed to be terrified for his life, turned out in their hundreds to greet them, six miles from the city boundary.

The Glasgow magistrates were never brought to trial despite urgent proddings from London. Witnesses were difficult to find, even against the ordinary people. The Lord Advocate said later, 'Consciences in this good country are so moulded that I can scarce find proof against any, but such as are fled . . . I had a notion that an oath hereabouts would have bore some weight and therefore I examined all on oath. But I find the tobacco trade has got much the better of the religion of the place.'[1] Some of the ordinary citizens were convicted and sentenced to be whipped by the public hangman and transported to the plantations. Eleven people appear to have been affected although an original move was made to prevent the Government from carrying out the sentences. This took the form of an indictment against the unhappy Captain Bushell and his brother officers. They were pardoned, however, and five of the rioters, at least, found their way to the colonies. The Town Council of Glasgow had to pay compensation of £6,080 sterling to Campbell of Shawfield. Ironically enough, the money came from an extra levy of 2d. on each pint of ale sold within the town.

The honourable bailies and citizens of Glasgow were not the only ones to suffer through these troubles. A more elevated victim was the Duke of Roxburghe, the Secretary of State for Scotland. He had opposed the tax and by means of it hoped to bring down Walpole's government. Walpole summed up the situation in his own words: 'The present administration is the first that was ever yet known to be answerable for the whole Government, with a Secretary of State for one part of the kingdom, who they are assured, acts counter to all their measures . . .'. He dismissed Roxburghe without appointing a successor, and the Secretaryship of State for Scotland lay fallow for six years. An unexpected benefit from the Malt Tax came in that a few thousand pounds of the revenue from it were set aside for improvements in the basically domestic linen industry in Scotland, at a time critical for that industry.

We can see the famous Porteous Riot of Edinburgh in 1736 as

having something in common with the Malt Tax troubles in Glasgow. There was the similar feature of communal discontent with the attempts to unify the Revenue systems of both countries. The riot was spawned in the aftermath of the execution of a smuggler. True, Wilson and Robertson in the eyes of the law were thieves as well as smugglers, but the crime for which they were convicted was the theft of £200 from a Customs House, that of Pittenweem. With Wilson's help, Robertson escaped from his guard while attending service in St Giles.

> Wilson who was a very strong fellow took Robertson by the head band of his breeks and threw him out of his seat, held a soger fast in each hand and one of them with his teeth, while Robertson got over and through the pews, pushed o'er the elder and plate at the door, made his way through the Parliament close, down the back stair, got out of the Poteraw gate before it was shut, the mob making way and fairly assisting him, got friends, money and a swift horse and fairly got off, nae mair to be heard of or seen.

So wrote Allan Ramsay, the poet and painter, in a letter to Duncan Forbes, the Lord Advocate. The sympathies of the populace which had speeded Robertson on his retreat were now with the remaining condemned man. Large numbers assembled on 14 April to witness the execution. The City Guard, under Captain Porteous, turned out to maintain order. There was no attempt to rescue Wilson before he was hanged, but afterwards some stones were thrown at the hangman. Porteous then fired into the crowd personally and ordered his men to do likewise. They dispersed the crowd quickly, leaving three men, one boy and one woman dead and a number wounded. He ordered another volley in a neighbouring street and killed some people on the third storey of a building.

The result of this apparently unprovoked killing was a great tenseness and resentment among the people. It is true that the City Guard must have been very much on edge themselves before the execution of Wilson, but now that that had been accomplished, there seems to have been no real need for such drastic action. The City Fathers were worried and uncertain and Porteous was imprisoned and ultimately tried for murder. He was condemned to death and the execution date was fixed for 8 September. There were important people, however, working for him and they interceded on his behalf. The result of their efforts was that Queen Caroline granted him a stay of execution of six weeks.

However, while Porteous was celebrating his good fortune with some friends in his Tolbooth cell on the eve of the execution day, a drum was beating in the Grassmarket and the mob was gathering. They overpowered the unsuspecting City Guard and secured the city gates. They forced the gates of the Tolbooth and captured Porteous. With some rope they bought in a shop in the Grassmarket, they hanged the former Captain of the City Guard just before midnight.

This riot in Edinburgh caused an even greater tumult in the corridors of Westminster than did the Glasgow riots. It was, however, basically the same situation; Queen Caroline was affronted and the Royal reprieve so assiduously obtained by men of influence was cast aside by a mob in a northern city. The reaction of the Government was sharper than in the case of Glasgow in that they brought in a Bill of 'Pains and Penalties' with the object of imprisoning the Lord Provost and bailies of Edinburgh and preventing them from ever holding office again, abolishing the City Guard, and demolishing the Nether-bow Port. The Bill was said to have been introduced at the instigation of Queen Caroline herself and indeed it does seem to have had something of feminine bitchiness about it. It survived a rough passage in the Houses of Lords and Commons, and resurfaced in a very much amended form. Lord Provost Wilson was prohibited from holding office as a magistrate and the city was fined £2,000, the money to be handed over to the widow of Captain Porteous. The Porteous Riot was confined to the act of murder by the mob execution of a condemned man and did not extend beyond the means necessary for this end. It can be seen as an organized and savage gesture of discontent against edicts issued by a distant administration.

Paradoxical as it may seem, any account of the history of Scotch whisky, particularly in the eighteenth century, is not complete without some reference to the situation in England. Historically and traditionally, the Englishman's drink was his beer. Information about distilling in England in mediaeval times is as scant as in Scotland. It is said that English armies invading Scotland would refuse to march if their beer ships were delayed. Wine drinking was more or less confined to the well-off, while spirit drinking, except for medicinal purposes, was rare. In the earlier period this would be the spirit of the grape, imported as such, or distilled locally from imported wine.

It is not that the English did not experience an addiction to spirits. In their campaigns in western Europe, they found fortification in brandy, or later and more thoroughly, in Dutch Geneva, or Hollands. While Burns neatly puts his finger on the traditional battle stimulant of the Highland soldier:

> Bring a Scotsman frae his hill
> Clap in his cheeks a Royal gill . . .

the Englishman found his 'Dutch courage' in the fruits of the experiments of Professor Sylvius of Leyden. As one writer put it 'they preferred to go to perdition in their own way'. Born, as whisky probably was, in the scientific atmosphere of medical chemistry, the English found the juniper-flavoured spirit very palatable. It was distilled initially from grain, usually rye, and then redistilled, or rectified, together with the essence of juniper berries. This new and suddenly popular spirit was called 'Geneva', after the French word *genièvre* – juniper, and later characteristically abbreviated to 'gin'.

As in Edinburgh earlier with the Barber Surgeons, the

15

English Worshipful Company of Distillers was formed and acquired a monopoly of distilling, this time within a twenty-mile radius of the City of London. King Charles I granted these rights, and distillation was to be carried on according to the written instructions of the two Royal Physicians, Dr. Thomas Cademan and Sir Theodore de Mayerne. Distilling had been carried on in England earlier in the century but in a crude way. Dregs of wine, sour beer, bad fruits, spices and drugs of various kinds only too often found their way into the wash. Perhaps it is not too fanciful to see behind King Charles' move motives similar to those which prompted his ancestor, James IV of Scotland, to grant similar rights to the Barber Surgeons of Edinburgh almost a century and a half before. The appointment of the two Royal Physicians as advisers is significant in indicating an interest in control over a substance that was regarded as a medicine. Though the terms of the Scottish legislation are vaguer, we see religion interweaving with the mystical science of alchemy and with medicine. In England, after the dissolution of the monasteries in the previous century, many monks set themselves up as distillers and apothecaries. We thus see the divinely bestowed science of distillation leaving the cloisters, becoming the skill of the layman, and falling victim ultimately to his control and to his legislation.

Other charters granting the right to distil were granted by Charles II and by James II. But the new industry did not blossom in England. The policies of these rulers were pro-French and the native product could compete but poorly against the finer brandy which came into the country in large quantities. This all changed with the 'Glorious Revolution' of 1688. The policy of William was decidedly anti-French. His Parliament from 1690 onwards imposed statutes which made it virtually impossible to import French brandy. They encouraged anyone to distil, 'any Law, Charter, or any other thing to the contrary notwithstanding'. In his enthusiasm to levy commercial warfare against the French, Dutch William can be said

to have inaugurated the inglorious revolution in English social
and drinking habits which culminated in the Gin Age. English-
made spirits from home-grown corn were the drinks of the true
patriot. Distillers were free to open as many retail spirit shops
as they chose, and the Government was proud to say that those
who set up distilling works in 'English Brandy' consumed annu-
ally 'great quantities of the worst sort of malted corn'. By the
turn of the eighteenth century the English were confirmed
drinkers of the hopefully named 'English Brandy'. Patriotic
jingoism, combined with the anaesthetization of the palate,
combined to kill the desire for French brandy even if it were
freely obtainable. In the words of Daniel Defoe, the distillers
had 'found a way to hit the palate of the poor by their new-
fashioned compound waters called Geneva, so that the common
people seem not to value the French brandy as usual, and even
not to desire it'. The law permitted gin to be sold almost any-
where. Retailers of groceries, hardware and other commodities
added the 'strong waters' to their wares. An apt statement from
Theophilus in the *Gentleman's Magazine* sums up the situation:
'one half of the town seems set up to furnish poison to the other
half'.

We now come to the age of the saying of 'Drunk for a penny,
dead drunk for tuppence.' Two historians agree as to which date
the true Gin Age commenced. Dr. Short picked the year 1724
as the year in which gin 'began to diffuse its pernicious effects',
and W. E. H. Lecky finds that it was in the same year that 'the
passion for gin drinking appears to have infected the masses of
the population and spread with the rapidity and violence of an
epidemic. . . . The fatal passion for drink was at once and
irrevocably planted in the nation.' There had been an eightfold
increase in gin production since 1690, and from an estimated
output of half a million gallons in that year, the gin factories by
1729, the year of the first anti-gin Act, had boosted their output
to nearly five million gallons. According to a survey made three
years later, one house in six in London was licensed to sell

alcoholic drink. The 'anti-gin' Act of 1729 had forced retailers to take a licence and had imposed a tax on gin itself. The intended effects of the Act were easily evaded and 'Parliament Brandy' was born. Legislation against drink had already had a long history of inefficacy, and yet the Act of 1733 which repealed that of 1729, actually prevented the sale of spirits outside dwelling houses. Thus dwelling houses became drinking shops:

> Vice thus abused demands a nation's care
> This calls the church to deprecate our sin
> And hurls the thunder of our laws on gin.

The thunder of laws continued, although not perhaps because of Pope. The administrators of law and justice in the county of Middlesex petitioned Parliament in 1736, pointing out that the 'drinking of geneva and other distilled waters had for some years greatly increased; that the constant and excessive use thereof had destroyed thousands of his Majesty's subjects; that great numbers of others were by its use rendered unfit for useful labour, debauched in morals and drawn into all manner of vice and wickedness'. The resultant Act of the year was obviously based on the thought that the low price of the thing was the trouble, that small amounts repeatedly available was the cause of drunkenness, and that the remedy was to remove both these conditions by a special tax. Retail of spirits was forbidden in quantities of less than two gallons without a licence costing £50. A duty of £1 a gallon was also imposed.

Many people had apprehensions about legislation of this kind and these were quickly realized. As the conditions of the impending Act became known to the public, serious riots broke out. In some cases these were blamed on the Jacobites. Prime Minister Walpole called out the Guards against the mob in London. Ironically enough he had been against the Bill. On their last day of freedom, the crowds of London pawned their clothes to get at the last of the cheap gin from shops which were clad in mourning. The Act failed by reason of its inability of enforcement. The Earl of Islay commented: 'The poor had run gin mad, and the rich had run anti-gin mad, and in this fit of madness no one would give an ear to reason.' Enforcement of the Act had to depend on common informers. The failure of this legislation was not due to any skilful evasion of it by manufacturers and retailers, but by open transgression. Informers did not dare to inform, and even magistrates dared not punish. One direct result was a deterioration in the quality of the already inferior gin, and the public hawking of it disguised as colic or gripe waters. A number of names were used to indicate the real content of the bogus medicine bottles – Make Shift, My Lady's Eyewater, the Last Shift, Old Tom etc. It was a former government informer against the transgressors of this law who sold the last-named liquor. Since the prisons were full he thought he would try the game himself in an original way. He nailed the sign of a cat to his window and attached a pipe. Thirsty pedestrians got the invitation to whisper to the cat – 'puss, give me tuppence worth of gin' and put the money in the cat's mouth. The gin then came pouring out.

Another result of the Act of 1736 was a great increase in the consumption of gin, and a great decrease in the income of the revenue. In seven years only two distillers took out licences at the fees which were required, and in the first two years only a few of 12,000 fines imposed on convicted persons were paid. The 'odious and contemptible' law had to be repealed, and repealed it was in 1742. It was reckoned that the consumption of gin had increased during the period of virtual prohibition from thirteen and a half million gallons to nineteen million gallons. Moderation was the principle of the new legislation and those who supported it claimed that 'a moderate dram' even of this 'pernicious' liquor was not a crime or sin. A reasonable revenue was imposed on manufacture, putting a reasonably high price on the spirit – the beginning indeed of the modern attitude to legislation of this kind. It is interesting, however, to note a return of the medical lobby in regard to the necessity of dram taking.

Lord Bathurst declared that 'whatever some abstemious and whimsical physicians may say others will tell you that a moderate dram of some spirituous liquors or other, or in what these terms is called a cordial, is necessary upon many occasions for the relief or support of nature'. The prevailing climatic conditions made such an aid to nature very necessary.

Our digression into the gin industry is not irrelevant to a study of whisky. While Scottish spirit duties had come into line with those of England at the Union of the Parliaments in 1707, they diverged in 1736. This stringent Act exempted Scotland. It was aimed at curing a social malady that was peculiarly English. Any similar malaise did not obtain in Scotland. Whisky seems to have graduated slowly and gently from being the drink of the lower classes to being everybody's drink. There was no sudden and massive appearance of cheap drink as in England when King William began his commercial fencing with the French.

Notes to chapter

[1] Referring to the increasing prosperity of Glasgow as a tobacco port at this period.

3
Convivial Society

The Songs

The type of society to be found in the Highlands and Islands of
Scotland in the late mediaeval and early modern period was
quite different from the societies developing in other parts of
western Europe at the time. It is true that the Highlands were
mountainous and difficult of access, but the physical isolation
of units of population defined by mountains, fiords and seas
was not itself the cause of the independent clan which was the
basis of Highland society. The derivation of the word 'clan' is
the Gaelic *clann* – and presupposes in its social use a real, or at
least, a strongly imagined, blood kinship. The parcels of territory defined by mountain range or sea were thus not occupied
by communities whose unity was based on belonging to that
particular area. Their patriotism had this further reference to
this kinship within the group. We cannot see a contest between,
say, MacLeods and MacDonalds in the same light as a Shrove-
tide affray between 'Uppies' and 'Doonies' in the streets of
Jedburgh, where the position of the Market Cross determined
the adversaries. It is really an affray between two opposing
sets of 'kith and kin'.

The main allegiance of these clans was to themselves. The
overall authority, whether of Scotland, or later, the United
Kingdom was an alien one, disrespected and unable to impose

its jurisdiction. Vicious cross-currents of feuding were ever-present and when the chiefs felt they were wronged, they did not wait for the cumbersome processes of Edinburgh law to bring them restitution. It was a heroic, almost a pagan society, a community in which the poet and harper were honoured and endowed with land. Ideals of bravery, generosity, and learning were cherished, and the internal cohesion of the clan was frequently strengthened by the chief and his personal retinue moving among the people on their traditional circuits, feasting and drinking at various points within the clan territories.

Throughout the last few documented centuries, and un-doubtedly previously, drink occupied a peculiar place in High-land society. Many of the earlier songs which still survive traditionally, mention drinking and indicate a special attitude to it. This does not mean that they are bacchanalian songs. They are mostly eulogies, praising the capacity of the chiefs in, among other things, feasting and drinking. Feasting and drinking appear as heroic activities mentioned in the same breath as steering a boat in storm or lifting a prey from the Lowlands.

Direct praise of the chief in this way led to his trying to live up to the name that the song-makers gave him; he rode and he fought, he sailed the seas to lift prey from the mainland and from Ireland, and he gave mammoth binges. When the bard MacVurich visited Chief Rory MacLeod at Dunvegan, he found that 'drinking was not a dream' at the castle, and he commemorated his six nights' stay:

Se hoidhche dhamhsa 'san Dun. . . .

Six nights have I been in the castle
In truest feasting;
We had strong drink in plenty
In a crowded fortress of wine.

With the cry of the harp and the loaded cups
Hatred and treachery are not found;

22

Laughter of fair-haired young men,
Inebriating ale round a blazing fire.

MacVurich's testimony about his being 'twenty times drunk
every day' at Dunvegan Castle at the turn of the seventeenth
century, or later for that matter, does not point to a novel or
unusual episode. Wild carousals were the rule when the supplies
of drink were adequate. The communal binge was glorified,
feast-giving in which both the capacity to drink and the means
to provide it are extolled:

> M'eudail, m'eudail, Mac 'ic Ailein
> Pòiteir an fhion air gach cala
> Ceannachadair fial nan galan.
> Mar dh'òlas càch, paighidh Ailean.

> I love Clanranald,
> Drinker of wine in every harbour,
> Generous buyer of gallons –
> As others drink, Alan pays.

The MacDonalds of Clanranald appear frequently in songs of
praise which have been handed down by tradition as being
unusually open-handed with their wine, and descriptions of
them can be imaginative:

> Dalta nam bard 's na mnathan gil' thu
> Ogha an fhir o'n Chaisteal Thioram. . . .

> Fosterling of poets and pure women
> Grandson of the man from Castle Tirrim
> You will make the hogsheads flow –
> Not with mean pool water,
> But with proud wine pouring –
> With shimmering wine in perfection.

The Clanranalds seem to have lived up to it; there is a saying
current in parts of the Hebrides about an eighteenth-century

chief: *dh'òl Mac 'ic Ailein na seachd stàitean* – 'Clanranald drank seven estates'.

These convivial binges undoubtedly were a forum for the plotting of raids and insurrections. Boasts would be made that old scores would be settled and the ever-ready song-maker was there to remind his chief that these were made:

> And when you turn your ship to land
> There will be strife about the harbour
> The blood of three kings will flow –
> The blood of MacNeil and Clanranald
> And the blood of the young Lord of Lochnell.

It is not surprising that the great communal drinking bouts of the Hebridean chiefs and their consequences attracted the attention of the legislators in Edinburgh. The Statutes of Iona, drawn up in 1609, formulated laws to put some sort of control over this situation:

> . . . one of the special causes of the great poverty of the Isles, and of the great cruelty and inhuman barbarity which has been practised by sundry of the inhabitants upon their natural friends and neighbours, has been their extraordinary drinking of strong wines and aquavitae brought in among them, partly by merchants of the mainland and partly by traffickers from among themselves.

It was ordered that no native of the Isles should import wine or 'aqua vitae', and that any native purchasing such goods from merchants on the mainland should be punished with heavy fines 'without prejudice to any person within the same Isles to brew aquavitae and other drink to serve their own houses'. Barons and other gentlemen of substance were given permission to send to the Lowlands for wine to serve their own houses.

The Statutes sought basic changes in the way of life of the Isles. They were far-sighted, although revolutionary for the time, in that they called for the establishment of inns. The laws of hospitality of the time in the Highlands required that all strangers must be entertained with food and welcome and they encouraged much abuse. In insisting that the chief should have a fixed place of residence, the Statutes were striking at the internal cohesion of the clan unit; they were discouraging the practice of the chief's 'circuit'. This convivial tour throughout the clan's territories could last months at a time if the territories were extensive. They were also aimed against the bards and appear to be echoing Spenser's strictures in Ireland on 'those which are to them instead of poets':

> ... of a most notorious thief and wicked outlaw, which had lived all his time of spoyles and robberies one of their Bardes in his praise said, that he was none of those idle milke-soppes that was brought up by the fire-side, but that most of his dayes he spent in armes and valiant enterprises, that he did never eat his meate before he had wonne it with his sword, that he lay not slugginge all night in a cabben under his mantle, but used comonlie to keep others waking, to defend their lives, and did light his candle at the flames of their howses. . . .
>
> (*A View of the Present State of Ireland*)

It is obvious even from the traditional songs which have survived into the present day that the legislators of the Statutes were correct in their belief that the bards had an inflammatory influence in the closed society of the clan. They were present at all the convivial gatherings where they had a ready-made audience and also where their influence could reach the 'non-official' song-makers, particularly the women on the cloth-waulking boards. They praised the chiefs and their sons as their lovers and in similar heroic terms. The women also kept the embers of inter-clan animosities warm whenever they got the chance, usually accusing a member of a rival clan of poverty and the lack of ability to entertain. For instance, a

25

MacLeod woman might reply to her MacDonald antagonist:

> I replied as I should –
> Well I know the custom of the MacLeods,
> Wine being broached, ale being drunk
> And thrice-distilled liquor
> Pouring into stoups.

The government found it difficult trying to implement their edicts concerning the consumption of wine. An Act was passed in 1616 laying down the actual quantities which were to be allowed. Looking at this 'rationing' system from our own standpoint today, the Act seems to have generous provision, even for thirsty Hebridean chiefs. MacLeod of Dunvegan, MacDonald of Sleat, and MacLean of Duart were each allowed to buy four tuns at a time, just over a thousand gallons, and chiefs with lesser estates, though no lesser thirsts, such as Clanranald, were limited to three tuns each. Minor chiefs, such as MacKinnon of Strath in Skye and MacLean of Loch Buy in Mull, were only allowed one tun each.

The Act of 1616 had to be repeated again in 1622 when it seems that the Islesmen were still drinking to the 'brek of His Majestie's peace', and all shippers were again seriously warned not to convey any more wine to the islands than the quantities permitted by the earlier legislation.

It is curious that the Statutes of Iona expressly permitted the distillation of whisky. It seems clear that the compilers of the Statutes thought that wine was the great enemy and that whisky would never gain the universal acclaim of wine. It is difficult for us to appreciate this attitude today, although it is probable that legislation such as in the Statutes encouraged the spread of distilling. In the period which I am talking about, the seventeenth century in this case, and thoughout the first half of the eighteenth century and beyond, wine was the universal drink of the upper classes, indeed, of all classes when they could get it.

1. Rory Mor Macleod's drinking horn and cup, Dunvegan Castle, against the background of the Fairy flag.

The cup is made out of a solid piece of oak, embossed with silver and standing on four silver feet. It is 10½ in. in height. It was probably brought from Ireland during forays against Queen Elizabeth's troops.

The inscription is as follows:

Katherina ingen ni ui Niell uxor Johannis Meguighir principis de Firmanach me freri fecit. Anno Domini 1493. Oculi omnium in te spectant Domine et tu das escam illorum in tempore opportuno.

Katherine, the daughter of John MacGuire, chief of Fermanagh, caused me to make this, in the year of our Lord 1493. The eyes of all wait upon you O Lord: and you will give them meat in due season.

The horn is a large ox-horn rimmed with a silver band engraved with a Celtic pattern. It was the custom for the young heir to drain it when he became of age. The custom has been revived recently.

2. **Three men from Islay.** Whisky at the centre of folktale collecting.
In the centre of the picture is John Francis Campbell of Islay, the great
collector of Gaelic folktales. On the right, looking rather squiffed, is his
chief assistant Hector MacLean. On the left is Lachlan MacNeill, shoe-
maker.

For August 17th, 1870, Campbell's diary records, 'Went from Glasgow
to Paisley, and to No. 5 Maxwellton Street to Lachlan MacNeill, shoe-
maker; found him and Hector installed in a small public, both rather
screwed, Hector the worse. They have been at the tale of O'Kane's leg for
about a week, and Hector has made about 62 sheets of Gaelic x4=248, say
about 260 pages of foolscap.'

3. **The De'il's Awa' wi' th' Exciseman.** From an etching by Bryden.

The de'il cam fiddling through the toon,
And danced awa' wi' th' Exciseman,
And ilka wife cries, "Auld Mahoun
I wish ye the luck o' the prize, man!"

The de'il's awa', the de'il's awa',
The de'il's awa' wi' th' Exciseman;
He's danced awa', he's danced awa',
He's danced awa' wi' th' Exciseman.

4. **Auld Gudeman ye're a Drucken Carle.** From an etching by Walter
Geikie.

> Auld gudeman ye're a drucken carle,
> > drucken carle,
> A' the day long ye wink an' drink,
> > an' gape an' gaunt;
> O' sottish loons ye're the pink an' pearl,
> > pink an' pearl,
> > Ill-fared, doited, ne'er-do-weel.

Walter Geikie was born in Edinburgh in 1759, and became deaf and
dumb through illness at the age of two. His chief claim to fame rests on his
etchings of street characters in Edinburgh.

The verse is from a poem by Sir Alexander Boswell, eldest son of the
famous biographer. He was killed in a duel at Auchtertool in Fife in
March, 1822.

This thirst-imposing legislation was unpopular. Perhaps the chiefs reflected on the Gaelic couplet:

Is bochd an deireadh beatha bròn
Is olc an deireadh òil padhadh.

Sorrow is a wretched end to life
Thirst is an evil end to drinking.

Or perhaps they simply yielded to a temptation which was natural to them to plunder shipping using Hebridean routes, but in any case there appears to be an increase in acts of piracy about this time. In simple terms, if the government of the country would not let them have as much wine as they wanted to buy, they would take it by force. The galleys of MacNeil and Clanranald ranged the seas between Ireland and Scotland looking for likely prey. The MacNeils seized a ship from Bordeaux off the coast of Barra, and in 1625, in the same area, Clanranald boarded a ship from Leith laden with wine and tea. About the same time, wine from a Burntisland ship taken in the Minch was broached and drunk in Dunvegan castle. Again in 1636, Clanranald seized an English ship, the *Susannah*, laden with a cargo of wine and fruits. This ship was a little off course and was 'salvaged' by Clanranald. On this occasion the chief made a slight pretence at legality; he forced the captain to sign a document 'selling' him the ship. Clanranald valued the ship at eight pounds.

While drink played a great part in the peculiar society of the clan system, and while numerous references to it occur both in the records of the Privy Council and in the surviving song literature of the period, it is difficult to trace a drinking or bacchanalian song from a period earlier than the eighteenth century. There is as yet no preoccupation with the nature or the psychological effects of drink, and apart from references to quality and purity, there is no detailed description of the actual drink. These marks of the true drinking song seem to be absent from Gaelic tradition earlier than the eighteenth century, when the praise of drink became a popular theme among poets. This coincided with the beginning of the era of heavy spirit drinking in the Highlands. Whisky became socially acceptable while brandy and Geneva were also used widely. This was the age of poetic analysis of drink. The Jacobite poet Alasdair Mac-Donald, for instance, in his 'Royal Song of the Bottle' dwells in detail on the effect of drink on character. The 'lover of thousands' will make the silent and the dour fluent, the bashful, amorous, while the shy will find the urge to dance thrust into their feet; whisky will make the miser generous and the churl a gentleman. MacDonald describes its appearance with minute visual and oral imagery; its bustling noise entering the drinking cup is sweeter to him than all the bells of Glasgow city, and the true welcome to brighten his mind is *mac na braich a teachd le pòig*.

At this period of predominantly spirit drinking in Scotland, other spirits came in for praise too. Duncan Ban MacIntyre, a poet active in the latter part of the eighteenth century, composed a song in praise of brandy. Both Geneva and brandy find some praise in a waulking song from Lewis from approximately the same period, and a Barra song says:

> *Chan e n' t-uisge beatha bh'ann*
> *Ach ruma mar a chaitheamaid*
> *An t-uisge làidir reamhar*
> *A ghabhadh air na h-éibhlean.*

> It was not whisky we had
> But rum to repletion,
> The strong thick spirit
> That would burn on embers.[1]

Geneva, however, gets very little praise in tradition, rather the reverse. This verse is from a folksong from the isle of Uist in praise of whisky:

Cha teid mi'n tigh sheinnse ud thall
Cha d'fhiach an sineubhair a th'ann
Ged chuir inn an togsaid ri'm cheann
Cha chuireadh e moille 'nam chainnt.

I will not go to yonder inn
Its Geneva is worthless
Though I'd put the cask to my head
My speech wouldn't falter.

The great popularizer of bottle-poetry in the Lowlands was undoubtedly Robert Burns. He was perhaps the first Scottish poet to realize that whisky was becoming the national drink of Scotland. In doing so, he makes it clear that he was in touch with the tides of legislation of his period relating to distilling and that he was aware of their inimicality to Scottish interests. The tightening of the Excise laws in 1785–6 and the intensified activity of Excise officers from that period were causing national concern. Burns expressed this concern in poetry of a high order and virtually identified Scotland with whisky. His greatest composition on the subject of drink, 'The Author's Cry and Prayer', is not a song of tavern conviviality but a semi-satirical expression of the country's feelings that her birthright is being interfered with and that her representatives in London are inadequate to defend them. He appeals to them:

Paint Scotland greeting owre her thrissle
Her mutchkin-stoup as toom's a whistle,
An' damned excisemen in a bustle,
      Seizin' a stell,
Triumphant crushin't like a mussel
      O lampit shell,

and asks:

Is there, that bears the name of Scot
But feels his heart's bluid rising hot,
To see his poor auld mither's pot

> Thus dung in staves,
> And plundered o' her hindmost groat
> By gallows knaves?

He exhorts them to do everything in their power to get 'auld Scotland' back her kettle, and if the liberties of the whisky drinkers and distillers are not restored, he visualizes more militant action:

> An' Lord, if ance they pit her till't,
> Her tartan petticoat she'll kilt,
> An' durk an' pistol at her belt,
> She'll tak the streets
> An' rin her whittle to the hilt
> I' th' first she meets.

As in 'The Author's Cry', Burns's purpose in 'Scotch Drink' is more nationalistic than convivial or bacchanalian, and the whole effect of both poems is vastly comical. The life of the whole nation is identified with John Barleycorn, and without him all activities would cease to function. He is at once the basis of physical well-being and the inspiration of the poet:

> On thee aft Scotland chows her cood,
> In souple scones, the choice of food;
> Or tumbling in the boiling flood
> Wi' kail an' beef;
> But when thou pours thy strong heart's blood,
> There thou shines chief.
> . . . .
> O Whisky, soul o' plays and pranks,
> Accept a Bardie's gratefu' thanks!
> When wanting thee what tuneless cranks
> Are my poor verses!
> Thou comes – they rattle i' their ranks
> At ither's arses.

In thus speaking for the nation, Burns becomes the national poet of Scotland and whisky becomes its national drink. In mood they are far removed from the alcoholic abandon of:

> It is the moon – I ken her horn,
> That's blinking in the lift sae hie;
> She shines sae bright tae wile us hame
> But by my sooth, she'll wait a wee!
>
> We are na fou, we're nae that fou
> But just a drappie in our ee;
> The cock may craw, the day may daw'
> And aye we'll taste the barley bree.

Burns is justly famous for his songs in which love, drinking and sentiments of lasting friendship are mingled and the whole English-speaking world knows at least a verse and chorus of 'Auld Lang Syne'. Although he disowned authorship of the song and said, 'Light be the turf on the breast of the heaven-inspired poet who composed this glorious fragment; there is more fire of native genius in it than in half a dozen of modern English bacchanalians', he is now generally regarded as the author of at least most of it. He certainly achieved skill in his 'pint of wine' love songs, and these would require a separate study. I would like to leave this particular topic with a quotation from a Highland swain who seemed to be willing to add yet another sickness to the one he already had:

> 'S mi gun òladh is gum paigheadh
> Dh'òlainn a ghaoil do dheoch-slàinte,
> A dh'fhion no bhranndaidh na Spàinne
> Ged a dh'fhàgadh e mi tinn.
>
> I would drink and I would pay
> I would drink, my love, a toast to you
> In wine or brandy from Spain
> – Though it would make me sick.

Why a convivial character such as Burns became an Exciseman in the later years of his life is a question which is often
asked. In his day, the Exciseman was almost beyond the pale.
Besides intoxicating liquors and other luxuries, many ordinary
household necessities were taxed, such as salt, sugar, window
glass, tallow candles and other things. The Exciseman was
despised by all classes and by teetotallers as well as drinkers.

Yet this convivial and gifted person became such a government employee. His intention at first seems to have been to
combine the life of a farmer with that of a part-time Exciseman,
but the farm proving unprofitable, he became a full-time officer
of Excise at the end of 1791.

It is to this period that we owe the delightful song 'The
Deil's awa' wi' th' Exciseman'. The imaginary illustration of this
event which we reproduce is by the Scottish artist Bryden.
There are different accounts as to the circumstances of the
composition of the song, one being that it was composed extempore by Burns at a convivial gathering of his fellow Excisemen at Dumfries. On being called for a song at this meeting,
Burns scribbled the verses on the back of a letter and handed
them to the chairman.

The generally accepted one comes from his biographer
Lockhart and is connected with the incident of the smuggling
brig *Rosamund*. She was seen aground in the shallow waters of
the Solway Firth while Burns was serving in the area, and he
went with some men to keep watch on the well-armed vessel.
Two others, Lewars and Crawford by name, were sent to
Dumfries and Ecclefechan for reinforcements. Impatient with
the delay in the return of Lewars, Burns was heard to say that
he wished the devil had him. It was accordingly suggested to
him that he should compose a song on the delay in the meantime.
The poet then apparently took a few steps among the reeds and
shingle and returned to sing the song.

Both accounts emphasize the extempore nature of the composition and indeed it is a very successful one. Dr. Johnson would

undoubtedly have approved of the song and indeed of Bryden's illustration. His *Dictionary* definition of 'Excise' is: 'A hateful tax levied upon commodities, and judged not by the common judges of property, but by wretches hired by those to whom Excise is paid.'

The eulogists of strong drink inevitably had their opponents. These did not necessarily come from advocates of complete temperance or from religiously minded people. The following verses are from a song composed by Lachlan MacPherson of Strathmasie, a friend of James 'Ossian' MacPherson, and described by his editor J. H. MacKenzie as 'having the felicity of expressing himself in terms most appropriate to the posture and light in which men stood, who exposed themselves to censure'. His subject was the convivial drinking group, or the 'Whisky Band':

> *Fear mo ghaoil an t-uisge beatha*
> *Air am bi na daoin' a feitheamh*
> *'S tric a chuir e saoidh 'nan laighe*
> *Gun aon chlaidheamh rusgadh.*

> *Ciod eile chuireadh sunnd oirrn*
> *Mar cuireadh bean is liunn e?*

A man of my heart is whisky
They all wait on him
He has often felled heroes
Without unsheathing a sword.

> What else can make us happy
> If women and drink cannot do it?

You will get the strongest hands there
And who better than the country lads?
Even a man at the urine runnel[2]
Could fell three of them.

33

They are full of courage and strength
Spirited and quick in action;
Twenty of them at that time
Would crown red-haired Charlie.

Though Martinmas dues remain unpaid,
Though the King should mount his mother,
They will drink their healing balm
Till their sinews weaken.

(From MacKenzie, J. H. (ed.), *Beauties of Gaelic Poetry*, 1904)

This song of twenty-one verses by the 'gentleman and scholar' of Strathmasie is merely an extended lampoon directed at the clamorous group who cannot hold their liquor. It is not a true didactic poem directed against drink. Didactic, or moralizing songs, do not seem to have a tenacious life in Gaelic folklore and they are by no means plentiful. The following verses speak in the person of the 'son of malt' himself, boasting of his power over men. He is the proud conqueror of millions, helping to place the rope round their necks and making their kinsfolk weep and wail. He speaks disparagingly of the various unwholesome substances of which he is made, and declares that, despite all, he will be sought after and carried around in a jar.

> *O na cur cùl rium*
> *Gur sunndach an gille mi,*
> *Idir na biodh nàir ort*
> *A ghràidh tigh'n 'gam shireadh-sa,*
> *'S gad a thug mi bàs*
> *Air do chàirdean tha fios agad,*
> *Aig àm na Bliadhn' Uire*
> *Gun giùlain thu 'm pige mi. . . .*

O do not reject me,
I am a merry youth,
Do not be ashamed, my dear,

34

To come seeking me,
And although I have given death
To your kinsfolk, you know
That at New Year
You will carry me in a jar.

I am a noble man
Who subdues millions,
I help to place the rope
Round their necks;
I drown some of them
Without putting a hand to any
And I make their kinsfolk
Weep and blubber.

And the smith in the smithy
Would pawn his anvil
To find the place
From where I come,
And the wright
His claw hammer to seek me,
And the mason his trowel
Though he would bewail it later.

And the weaver and the clerk
Doughty men,
They leapt at each other
Their shirts in ribbons,
Such blood in their noses
Gladdened my heart,
Their feet through their shoes
Their buttocks through their breeks.

If you understood my nature
You would not give a penny for me;

I am made
Of soap and mud;
If you understood my nature
You would never buy me,
I have a little of the 'blue stone'
Many a thing it contains.

O do not reject me
I am a merry youth;
Do not be ashamed, my dear,
To come seeking me,
And although I have given death
To your kinsfolk, you know
That at New Year
You will carry me in a jar.
(Translated from the singing of Miss Nan MacKinnon,
Isle of Vatersay, Barra)

The clergy in Scotland were not by any means as opposed to drinking and smuggling as they would like the public to believe. Certainly, intemperance and trafficking in uncustomed goods were condemned openly, but we find from the minutes of early synod meetings that the ministers themselves were frequently men of the world in these matters. The Reverend Aeneas MacAulay of Gairloch was accused by his synod in 1754 of buying a quantity of rum and Geneva from a boat in the smuggling trade and selling it to his parishioners. We find that the Reverend Archibald Campbell of Morven was accused of being drunk at a baptism in 1733. Speaking in his own defence, he admitted to having been in a state of *corra-ghleus*, which he explained as being 'no more than that cheerful humour which a moderate glass puts into one'. We read a complaint from a Mr. Chisholm, newly ordained in Kintail in 1720, that one Murdo MacRae, with a band of his fellow clansmen, 'besett the manse, broke down the doors, went to his bed-chamber, cut and tore his bed-hangings and his bed-clothes, pursued the minister, who escaped naked out of the window, firing at him – and did plunder and carry off thirty gallons of whisky from the manse'. This pathetic complaint prompts the question as to what the good minister was doing with thirty gallons in his manse. It may be that he had taken it upon himself to confiscate uncustomed goods and that Murdo MacRae and his confederates were merely recovering them.

Perhaps the attitude of the Church to the illegality or sin of smuggling or illicit distilling is best seen in its castigation of its own parishioners. All too frequently the crime of smuggling is felt to be seen merely as a breach of the Sabbath, smuggling or distilling in an ordinary way and doing so on Sunday being two different matters. Wood in his *Smuggling on the Solway* tells of a classic example of violent smuggling being regarded simply as a breach of the Sabbath which may be found in the minutes of a meeting held by the session of the joint parishes of Colvend and Southwick on 10 May 1741. The meeting was held because of a case of smuggling which occurred on the previous Sunday. The Excise officers had seized a quantity of smuggled goods belonging to a William Lindsay. Lindsay then gathered some of his friends and attacked and injured some of the officers. The group, seven in all, appeared before the session and confessed privately to their Sabbath breaking. They requested that they should not be publicly rebuked as this would help the civil authorities in any case they would bring against them. The session agreed.

Dr. Alexander Webster, minister of Tolbooth Kirk and leader of the Evangelicals or 'Highflyers', who later became the Free Church of Scotland, may be claimed to have been the most noted drinker in the Protestant Church in Scotland. He was a man of sincere piety but at the same time he was regarded as the most noted toper and boon companion in eighteenth-century Edinburgh. He was a man of such great business ability that he was being constantly consulted by the City Fathers in the town's affairs. It was said that he had drunk enough claret at the town's expense to sink a seventy-four-gun ship.

Visitors and Natives

Scotland has had a good share of comment by literary travellers, commonly English. 'Knocking' the Scots was a favourite English diversion particularly in the eighteenth century, and there is no lack of comment of a sociological kind. The union between the two countries developed uneasily. This haphazard seventeenth-century union of one monarch with two separate administrations was little improvement on the armed separation of previous centuries. Both countries embroiled themselves in each other's religious conflicts and Scotland intervened in the English Civil War between King and Parliament, on the understanding (not fulfilled) that she would be given control of that country's ecclesiastical affairs.

One of the most splenetic accounts of Scotland in the seventeenth century was published in London in 1679. Although he did not append his name to it at the time, the author was Thomas Kirk of Cookridge, Yorkshire, whose *Journal* of a tour to Scotland was published later. The extreme animosity shown in the *Modern Account* is probably politically biased and may have been inspired by the treatment of King Charles I by the Scots. Here are some of Kirk's comments on Scotsmen and drink in the *Account*:

> Their drink is ale, made of beer-malt and turned up in a small vessel called a cogue; after it has stood a few hours they drink it out of the cogue, yeast and all; the better sort brew it in larger quantities and drink it in wooden quaichs. But it is sorry stuff, yet excellent for preparing bird lime; but wine is the great drink with the gentry, which they pour in like dishes, as if it were their natural element; the glasses they drink out of are considerably large, and they always fill them to the brim and away with it; some of them

38

have arrived at the perfection to tope brandy at the same rate; sure, these are a bowl above Bacchus and of right ought to have a nobler throne than a hogshead.

Kirk's *Journal* of his tour first appeared in print in 1830, as an appendix to the *Diary of Ralph Thoresby, FRS*, edited by Joseph Hunter. Thoresby had also travelled in Scotland and was a contemporary of Kirk.

While Kirk also makes caustic comments in his *Journal*, it is evident that by comparison with what he says in his *Modern Account*, that he was something of a hypocrite. While in Scotland he appears to have conducted something of a toper's pilgrimage, drinking heavily and regularly. True he did not like the ale in southern Scotland any more than that of Northumberland: 'the ale in this country is made of bigg-malt (i.e. a variety of winter barley) and is not gustful to our palates, nor was the ordering of their meat to us'. He found the wine in the country more 'gustful' however, and he notes that at Aberdeen it cost him a mark a pint. While in Banff, at the Laird of Meldrum's house, he drank considerably and appreciatively: 'this company drank four or five rummers of claret with two ladies'. With the sheriff of the town in a tavern called 'Bonnie-wife's', he records 'in half an hour we drank more wine than some of us could carry away'. Yet later in the afternoon he was treated with 'excellent good claret' at Huntly's house and 'we had our full doses of it'. He caroused in Elgin the following day, but being short of wine, he fell back on a bowl of punch. In Inverness he was treated heartily with 'ale and usquebah'. He complains of the drink in Kirkwall where the Provost treated him with 'ill ale and worse sack'. At Dunbeath Castle, the Laird, Sinclair, entertained them with 'deep glasses of beer till we were very merry'.

Scotland has had more than its share of dispraise from travellers. Kirk may have been a special case in that he appeared to have a built-in spleen against the Scots. Yet he was an observant traveller, and despite the poisonous distortion of the *Modern*

Account, we can see by the *Journal* that he went out of his way to gain information.

Edward, or Edmund, Burt can be compared to Kirk in many ways. He came to Scotland determined not to enjoy himself and only to find fault. He is a rather shadowy figure and although he was a close associate of General Wade during Wade's epic road-making activities in the Highlands, we are not sure whether he was a soldier or a civilian surveyor. Whatever he may have been, he left his own acidulous account of Scotland and particularly the Highlands in his *Letters from a Gentleman in the North of Scotland to his Friend in London*. The date of publication, 1754, is misleading, as the letters were actually written between 1725 and 1728.

Despite his bias, Burt was a close observer of society, and if we excuse his terror of anything dirty, his account of his travels can be informative. Poor Burt ran into trouble immediately he set foot in Scotland. He claims to have been overcharged on the horse ferry across the Tweed to Kelso, but could obtain no redress from the magistrates. He had a further setback at his inn in Kelso. He was offered potted pigeons, but when he came to examine them:

> there were two or three pigeons lay mangled in the pot, and behind were the furrows in the butter of those fingers that had raked them out of it, and the butter itself needed no close application to discover its quality. My disgust at this sight was so great, and being a brand new traveller, I ate a crust of bread and drank a pint of good claret.

It is significant that, despite their prejudices, English travellers could not find fault with the claret they found in Scotland. Even the splenetic toper Kirk was more or less satisfied with this beverage as he found it on his journey. In this light, the usually sagacious Dr. Johnson's remarks on board Uilinish's boat in Skye on the way to Talisker on 23 September 1773, sound boorish. According to Boswell, he was on his familiar theme of 'railing' at the Scots. He claimed that they were the 'only instance of a people among whom the arts of civil life did not advance in proportion with learning; that they had hardly any trade, money or elegance before the Union; that it was strange that, with all the advantages possessed by other nations, they had not any of those conveniences or embellishments which are the fruits of industry, till they came into contact with a civilized people'.

> 'We have taught you,' said he, 'and we'll do the same to all barbarous nations – to the Cherokees, – and at last to the Ouran-Outangs,' laughing with as much glee as if Monboddo had been present.' *Boswell*. 'We had wine before the Union.' *Johnson*. 'No, sir; you had some weak stuff, the refuse of France, which would not make you drunk.' *Boswell*. 'I assure you, sir, there was a great deal of drunkenness.' *Johnson*. 'No, sir; there were people who died of dropsies, which they contracted in trying to get drunk.' (Boswell, James, *Journal of a Tour to the Hebrides*, London, 1956, ed. Werner.)

Boswell did not add that the Scots had a knowledge of the chemistry of distillation.

Burt was no more content with the fare he got in the Highlands than he was in the Lowlands. Although he is always very chary of mentioning names, he seems to have been entertained at the houses of some of the chiefs. He describes one dinner which was almost certainly given by Simon Fraser, Lord Lovat, at Castle Dounie.

> Our entertainment consisted of a large number of dishes, at a long table, all brought in under covers, but almost cold. What the greatest part of them were I could not tell, nor did I enquire, for they were disguised after the French manner; but there was placed next to me a dish which

I guessed to be boiled beef. I say it was my conjecture, for it was covered all over with stewed cabbage, like a smothered rabbit, and over all a deluge of bad butter.

When I removed some of the encumbrance, helped myself and tasted, I found that the pot it had been boiled in had given it too high a gout for my palate, which is always inclined to plain eating.

I then desired one of the company to help me to some roasted mutton, which was indeed delicious, and therefore served for my share of this inelegant and ostentatious plenty.

We had very good wine, but did not drink much of it; but one thing, I should have told you, was intolerable, viz., the number of Highlanders who attended at table, whose feet and foul linen, I don't know which, were more than a match for the odour of the dishes.

The conversation was greatly engrossed by the chief before, at, and after dinner; but I do not recollect any-thing was said that is worth repeating.

There were as we went home several descants upon our feast; but I remember one of our company saying that he had tasted a pie, and that many a peruke had been baked in a better crust.

When we returned hither in the evening, we supped up-on beef-steaks, which some who complained they had not made a dinner, rejoiced over, and called them a luxury.

In this description, Burt sounds as though he is a member of a group of cross-Channel trippers returning from Calais. The castle he describes is undoubtedly Lovat's. Lovat had spent some thirteen years resident in France and he was well known for his exotic dishes and his skill at grading his guests at table. His biographer Hill Burton gives a good description of dinner at Castle Dounie:

5. **Amen Glass,** eighteenth century (see p. 53).
(From the National Museum of Antiquities of Scotland.)

6. **Jacobite Glass,** with coloured likeness of the
Young Pretender (see p. 53).

(From the National Museum of Antiquities of Scotland.)

Sir

Monday next is a day of the year with me hallowed as the ceremonies of Religion, and sacred to the memory of the sufferings of my King and my Forefathers. — The honour you do me by your invitation, I most cordially and gratefully accept. —

Tho' something like moisture conglobes in my eye,
Let no one misdeem me disloyal;
A poor, friendless Wanderer may well claim a sigh,
Still more if that Wanderer were royal.

My fathers that Name have rever'd on a throne;
My fathers have died to right it;
Those fathers would shun their degenerate son
That Name should he scoffingly slight it.

St James's sq.
Medn: even.

I am, Sir,
your obliged humble servt
Robt Burns

James Stewart Esqr

7. Burns's reply to James Steuart (see p. 54).
(*From the National Museum of Antiquities of Scotland.*)

8. Gill and Mutchkin measures, seventeenth century.
(*From the National Museum of Antiquities of Scotland.*)

At the long table at Castle Dounie the guests and the viands had a corresponding progression downwards. At the head of the table there were neighbouring chiefs and distinguished strangers, claret and French cookery graced the board. The next department was occupied by the Duine wassels (gentlemen of the clan), who enjoyed beef and mutton with a glass of some humbler wine. The sturdy commoners of the clan would occupy the next range, feeding on sheep heads, and drinking whisky or ale. In further progress the fare degenerated with the feeders, and, clustering on the castle green in sunshine, or cowering in the outhouses in foul weather, were the ragamuffins of the clan to gnaw bones and devour the other offal. It was a rule of the house that the day's provender, whatever it might be, should be consumed; and if the deerstalker or the salmon spearer had been more fortunate than usual, the rumour would spread fast enough to bring an immediate demand for the supply. The practice gave much temptation to the troop of servants who attended the table, to snatch away unfinished dishes and many amusing instances have been recorded, of the necessity of the guest at Castle Dounie preserving a ceaseless watch over his plate, and of the certainty of its instantly disappearing during any moment of negligence.

(*Lives of Lovat and Forbes*, London, 1847)

Like the wily schemer he was, Lovat had to be careful about the correctness of his gradations. The table was a forum of clan politics and alignments and also a suitable means for gleaning military intelligence from the local English garrisons. It was essential to remember the claims of individuals personally, and to justify his grading of them if that were necessary. It is understood that he had great skill in this matter and would quickly smooth the feelings of any poor relation who might be looking askance at his portion by saying: 'Cousin, I told my lads to give you claret, but I see you like ale better; here's to your roof-tree.'

Lovat was a close associate of the Forbes family of Culloden, and one of their chief antagonists. Duncan Forbes became Lord Advocate, President of the Court of Session, and a conscientious and unimaginative supporter of the Government. We know a great deal about them both since they were indefatigable letter writers and they were both known to Edward Burt.

Despite their opposing views as to the political future of the Highlands, their social habits were similar and the Forbes family were remarkably convivial entertainers even by Highland eighteenth-century standards.

Duncan's brother was Laird of Culloden prior to Duncan. He was known as 'Bumper John' to distinguish him from the other lairds. Burt was entertained by him at Culloden House and he calls him:

a gentleman whose hospitality is almost without bounds. It is a custom of that house, at the first visit or introduction, to take up your freedom, by cracking his nut, as he terms it, that is a cocoa shell which holds a pint, filled with champagne, or such other sort of wine as you may choose. Few go away sober at any time, and for the greatest part of his guests, in the conclusion, they cannot go at all.

This he partly brings about by artfully proposing, after the public healths, (which always imply bumpers) such private ones as he knows will pique the interest or inclinations of each particular person in the company, whose turn it is to take the lead, to begin it in a brimmer; and he himself being always cheerful, and sometimes saying good things, his guests soon lose their guard – and then – I need say no more.

As the company are disabled one after the other, two servants who are all the time in waiting, take up the invalids with short poles in their chairs, as they sit (if not fallen down) and carry them to their beds, and still the hero holds out.

I remember one evening, an English officer who has a great deal of humour, feigned himself drunk, and acted his part so naturally that it was difficult to distinguish it from reality; upon which the servants were prepared to take him up, and carry him off. He let them alone till they had fixed the machine, and then raising himself to his feet, made them a sneering bow, and told them he believed there was no occasion for their assistance, whereupon one of them said with a sang froid and a serious air – 'No matter sir, we shall have you by and by.'

(*Letters from the North*, 1, 135)

Duncan was only second to his brother Bumper John in his assiduous conviviality. It is remarkable that people in the forefront of the public life of the time could consume such quantities of claret. We have already mentioned such a public figure as Dr. Alexander Webster. Although regarded as a 'five-bottle' man and carrying the nickname of Dr. Bonum Magnum, it seemed to be quite in order that he should be leader of the Evangelical religious group. It is clear that hard drinking had nothing to do with moral and religious scruples. Letters passing between Duncan and his friends indicate the arduous nature of their festivities. Duncan describes a journey from Edinburgh to the north in the spring of 1715.

We jogged along cursing the tapped hens, and yawning out our real sorrow for parting.

Wednesday, 30th March. Awaked; query, a sore throat? Difficulty in swallowing a spittle; cursed all stoups down from the tapped hen to the half-gill. Rose up about nine; bathed in cold water; chaffed my throat with Hungary water; tried to apply Brandy inwardly but in vain, could drink no wine; walked about till twelve. Took horse fasting; was often asked by my cousin on the rode how I did. Could not answer without pain. Sung none. Had several wise reflections which almost came to Resolutions.

Shutting his lips against the air and against vows, he arrived in Cupar in Fife at three in the afternoon. He still found that he could not take a drink all day, although his teeth watered as he watched his cousin drink two bottles of wine. He was somewhat improved the following day. He found that he could speak and sing and swallow 'dramers'. He was quite his usual self the following day and he 'supped and rejoised over ten bottles at a friend's house'. He toped to excess on Sunday, 3 May, noting that he drank ten bottles of wine with some strong ale. He awoke on Monday morning somewhat indisposed. He drank some brandy with the Provost of Elgin and pegged his wine consumption at five pints. By Tuesday, seven days after he left Edinburgh, he reached Inverness to begin the local convivial round with relatives, local gentry and garrison officers.

Travellers estimated that Scotswomen at this period drank more than women in the south, and that they sometimes exceeded men in this propensity. In his *Recollections*, Alexander Carlyle records his tour of the border while a boy in company with his father and the Reverend Robert Jardine, minister of Lochmaben. They called at the house of Bridekirk to visit the laird, but they found that he was absent and they were greeted by Lady Bridekirk. Carlyle describes the meeting:

> I had never seen such a virago as Lady Bridekirk, not even among the oyster women of Prestonpans. She was like a sergeant of foot in women's clothes, or rather like an over-grown coachman of a Quaker persuasion. On our peremptory refusal to alight, she darted into the house like a hogshead down a slope, and returned instantly with a pint bottle of brandy, a Scots pint, I mean – and a stray beer flask, into which she filled almost a bumper. After a long grace said by Mr. Jardine, for it was the third bottle of

brandy we had seen since we left Lochmaben – she emptied it to our healths and made the gentlemen follow her example. . . . This lady was famous, even in the Annandale border, both at the bowl and in battle; she could drink a Scots pint of brandy with ease, and when the men grew obstreperous in their cups, she could either put them out of doors or to bed, whichever she found most convenient.

The hard toping of claret, whisky and brandy in eighteenth-century Scotland must have come as a shock to the constitutions of travellers weaned on the more genial conviviality of the south. Another convivial occasion of an unusual kind which they would be surprised to see would be the roup, or house-sale. While Mrs. Grant of Laggan cannot be regarded as a traveller, she was a voluminous writer of informative letters to friends and acquaintances in the south and is a good source of information on social customs in eighteenth-century Scotland.

Writing to a Miss Jane Ewing on 5 July, 1786, she says:

We here have all been in a hurry with public amusements for this fortnight past. You will be quite at a loss to conjecture what they can be. Roups, then are a great source of amusement here, and a very expensive one to the roup makers. At the dissolution of any family, by the death or removal of its head, it is the custom to send out letters of invitation to the connexions of the family in the neighbouring counties, inviting them to countenance the ceremony by their presence. This invitation tacitly includes an invitation warranted by old custom, that these allies, as they call them, will purchase things rather beyond their value. . . . Whether it can be well afforded or not, there is always a plentiful dinner, and very plentiful drink on these occasions. Besides the entertainment for the superior class, there is always a plentiful distribution of bread, cheese and whisky to the peasantry, whose cheerfulness never exceeds the bounds of respect and decorum. The good humour, diffused by this meeting of numbers, who know and like each other, though they do not often mingle, and the emulation of goodwill to the entertainers, generally raise things to a great price. Though you want nothing, you must appear to countenance the business. . . . The roup lasted a week. We had a cold collation there every day and as many strangers at our own house every night as it would manage.

The age of carousing and conviviality passed its heyday in Scotland in the eighteenth century. No longer do accounts from travellers or from within the country stress it to the same extent. It is true, however, that as late as the nineteenth century, William Cobbett, MP, who travelled in 1832, finds it necessary to boast: 'I verily believe that I shall be the first human being that ever came into Scotland, and went out of it again, without tasting wine, spirits, beer or cider.'

Sir John Carr directed his strictures not so much against drink as against whisky in particular. In his *Caledonian Sketches* published in 1809, he makes it clear that if he had his way he would have abolished whisky distilleries and substituted them with breweries of 'wholesome ale'.

The ingenuity of the Scotch could not be applied to the improvement of an art more pernicious and deletirious, and of one which presents, in a moral and physical point of view, a more shocking and efficaceous check to the improvement of the people. The different effects of whisky and ale upon the soldiers of the militia regiments have frequently been observed. Whisky produces anger with intoxication but ale generally good humour. . . . Happy would it be if these manufacturers of public poison be everywhere checked and breweries of wholesome ale encouraged in their room.

Robert Southey, then Poet Laureate, travelled in 1819 with the famous engineer Telford. Among the comments which he left us is a literary one on the homely Twopenny ale: 'When they watered the horses, they mixed meal with the water. We watered ourselves at the same time on luxurious Twopenny, which is bottled small beer, as weak as Mr. Locke's *Metaphysics*, as frothy as Counsellor Philip's eloquence, and when the cork has been drawn for a few minutes, as vapid as an old number of the *Edinburgh Review*.' We get a different assessment of this beverage in the book *Traditions of Edinburgh*, by Robert Chambers, published in 1825. Writing of the Wig Club, he says that it was remarkable for 'drinking the old Scottish Ale called Twopenny, upon which, we have heard the old people say, it was possible to get most satisfactorily drunk for a groat'.

While Southey reproves the Highlanders for carrying on an illicit trade with the Lowlands in contraband salt, his concern for the national exchequer does not extend to condemning the extensive traffic in illicit whisky which must have been at its peak at the time of his visit. While he could not condone the Highland custom which was then prevalent of having a glass of whisky before breakfast, it seems that he was quite partial to the spirit. His inn at Achanalt was 'a miserable place, bad as a Gallician posada, or an estallagem in Algarve. But we tasted whiskey here, which was pronounced to be of the very best and purest – unexcised by kings.' On the following day also he records his pleasure at tasting 'right Highland whiskey'. We can only say that Telford was a good guide.

One of the most famous of travellers in the Highlands has undoubtedly been Bonnie Prince Charlie and it is unfortunate that he did not leave his own account of his wanderings. It was during his months on the run that the ordinary Highland people met and on the whole liked him.

After the disaster of Culloden Charles fled westwards, rejecting the offer of the Highland army reassembled at the captured barracks of Ruthven, to continue the war. At this period of grave personal danger, it seems to be true that he showed few signs of sympathy for the straits in which he left his adherents and dependants. On 26 April 1746, he was taken to an eight-oared boat at Loch nan Uamh on the west coast of the county of Inverness, very near to the spot where Captain Durbe and the brig *Douteille* had brought him nine months previously. His life was now in the hands of an old man from the north coast of Skye, Donald MacLeod of Galtrigill, a skilful pilot. A violent storm drove them further westwards across the southern Minch to the island of Benbecula in the Outer Hebrides. Charles spent three days in a doorless cowhouse before leaving for Stornoway but he could get no help from the prudent people of that town. Still in the wardship of Donald MacLeod, the royal wanderer was forced to flee southwards to the shelter of another mean Benbecula bothy. But help came to him now from old Clanranald and Charles received food, shoes, stockings, Spanish wines and six clean shirts, as well as instructions to move to a more secure hiding place in South Uist.

At no time was he more accessible to visitors than the weeks he spent in comparative security and comfort at a primitive hunting lodge in Glen Coridale in South Uist. There, under the guardianship of Clanranald's men, he fished and hunted and drank openly with the natives who came to see him. This was the period during which the Highlanders' strange fidelity to the Prince was most marked. Although the hundreds who knew where he was also knew of the vast reward of £30,000 which was being offered for his person, only one, a hungry beggar boy who had been fed and clothed at the bothy, made any attempt to betray him. Fortunately, his story was not believed by the military. While the island was in imminent danger of being searched, MacDonald of Baleshare and MacDonald of Boisdale were appointed to warn him and to make plans for his future safety.

Baleshare left an account of this meeting with the Prince.

His dress was then a tartan short-coat and a vest of the same, got from Lady Clanranald; his night-cap all patched with soot-drops, his shirt, hands and face patched with the same; a short kilt, tartan hose and Highland brogues, his upper coat being of English cloth. He called a dram, being the first article of Highland entertainment, which being over, he called for meat. There was half a stone of butter laid on a timber plate, and near a leg of beef laid on a patch before us, all patched with soot-drops. . . . Boisdale told him there was a party come to Barra in search of him . . . and he said he was not in the least concerned. The Young Gentleman told us, as it was seldom he met friends he could enjoy himself with, he would on no account part with us that night. Boisdale says to me that we could not in good manners part with him that night. . . . The Young Gentleman advises Edward Burke to fill the bowl. Boisdale insists on his being shaved first and then putting on a clean shirt. Then we began with our bowl frank and free. As we were turning merry, we were turning more free. . . . We continued this drinking for three days and nights. He still had the better of us, even of Boisdale himself, notwithstanding his being as able a bowlsman, I daresay, as any in Scotland.

Charles was on the run again and after hairbreadth escapes, was furnished with a false passport and an outlandish disguise by Flora MacDonald. For his voyage to Skye Charles was dressed in a 'flowered linen gown, a light coloured quilted petticoat, and a mantle of dun camlet, made after the Irish fashion with a hood'. During his first night in Skye, he was sheltered by old MacDonald of Kingsburgh. With MacDonald, he drank toddy from a china punchbowl late into the night. Charles would not obey his host's advice to go to bed and get a decent night's rest, so they drank bowl after bowl. At length, Kingsburgh refused to make another although Charles insisted to such a degree that the punchbowl was broken in an attempt to take it from his host. Here the Prince slept in a proper bed for many weeks. Since most of the troops pursuing him at this time were concentrated in the Outer Isles, his passage through Skye was mainly without incident. He changed his strange garb for a kilt and plaid and visited Portree on his way to Raasay. He found this island thoroughly wasted by the soldiery with hardly a house habitable. Although while in Skye he was able to proceed without disguise here he had to conceal his true identity, and the account of his leaving Portree with a bottle of whisky tied to his belt at one side and a bottle of brandy at the other would not be unusual in a hard-drinking community. He managed to reach the MacKinnon country in the southern part of Skye, and a bodyguard of that people took him to the mainland where he had to endure further privations. He embarked ultimately in safety in September on the appropriately named French ship *L'Hereux*, at the now-familiar anchorage of Loch nan Uamh.

The story of Charles' five-month odyssey through the Highlands and Islands is a remarkable one. Despite a youth spent in luxury, he showed that he could endure the privations of a fugitive as well as any Highlander. If he made himself unpopular with the Highland chiefs during the campaign by the attentions he lavished on the unworthy courtiers who followed him, he seems to have become genuinely popular with the ordinary people who came to know him personally during his wanderings. His conviviality and his drinking capacity won him acceptance among a race to whom such propensities were heroic virtues.

Almost everyone who helped Charles was captured within a short time of doing so, although most of them were released after the Indemnity Act of June 1747. MacDonald of Kingsburgh came very near to execution while in prison in Fort Augustus and Edinburgh Castle. Flora MacDonald was imprisoned in London, although in somewhat better conditions, and Donald MacLeod was captured as well. To their efforts Charles certainly owed his life, and his oft-repeated statement about 'Providence' looking after him must have been a little irritating to those who did so much to protect him.

The failure of the rising brought legislation which was designed to make it impossible for the Highlanders ever again to threaten the government of the country by force of arms. All steps possible were taken to humiliate a proud race, even to the extent of arranging a procession of chimney-sweeps through the streets of Edinburgh, bearing fourteen captured clan banners to the Market Cross, there to be burnt by the common hangman. New measures were taken to suppress concealment of weapons, while the use of any article of the Highland dress was prohibited everywhere north of the Highland line.

Despite the failure of the greatest rebellion to date, the Jacobite cause still had its place in the convivial life of Scotland, and the birthday of the Prince was celebrated at privately held carousals. Specially manufactured Amen glasses, Jacobite propaganda goblets, circulated among the community for the drinking of the health of 'the King over the Water'. The Amen Glass shown in plate 5 is engraved with a Crown, the Royal Cipher, J.R. 8, for King James VIII of Scotland and III of England, and two verses of the Jacobite National Anthem, with Amen.

> God save the King, I pray
> God bliss the King I pray
> God save the King
> Send him Victorious
> Happy and Glorious
> SOON to reign over us
> God save the King.
>
> God bliss the Prince of Wales
> The true-born Prince of Wales
> Sent us by thee
> Grant us one favour more
> The King for to restore
> As thou has done before
> The Familie.
>   Amen.

53

The Jacobite Glass shown in plate 6 is engraved with a colour likeness of Prince Charles. Both of them have an interesting history. They were both used at parties held in the house of one James Steuart in Edinburgh, on 31 December each year to celebrate the birthday of Prince Charlie. Robert Burns was invited to attend the one held on 31 December 1787, and we show in plate 7 his letter of acceptance containing two verses of poetry. The verses themselves are those he used as the second and third verses of what is probably the worst poem he ever wrote, 'Poetical Address to William Tytler'.

> Tho something like moisture conglobes on my eye,
>   Let no one misdeem me disloyal;
> A poor friendless Wanderer may well claim a sigh,
>   Still more if that Wanderer were royal.

> My fathers that Name have rever'd on a throne,
>   My fathers have died to right it;
> Those fathers would spurn their degenerate son,
>   That Name should he scoffingly slight it.

The only difference between the verses in the poem and those on the glass occurs in the second line of the second stanza, where 'died' is written on the glass and 'fallen' in the poem. The 'Address to Tytler' was accompanied by a present of the bard's picture.

William Tytler was Laird of Woodhouselee and something of a Jacobite. In 1759 he published a book called *An Inquiry, Critical and Historical, into the Evidence against Mary Queen of Scots*. It ran into four editions. Why Burns chose to use these verses for two different occasions remains a mystery.

It was inevitable that as the century progressed, Jacobite sympathies should become the symptom of an ageing generation and that usually of the female sex. While the carousing continued year after year in the drawing-rooms of Edinburgh, the subject of a thousand toasts was lapsing into a petulant debauchery in Rome. Robert Burns had attended the last festivity of this kind to be held in the house of James Steuart in Edinburgh. The death of the Young Pretender a month later, on 30 January, removed for ever the focus of Jacobitism.

Drinking Vessels and Measures

When one explores the annals of conviviality in Scotland in the seventeenth and eighteenth centuries, one meets with a number of vessels used for drinking: bickers, stoups, mutchkins etc. The range can be quite confusing, and one way to sort out at least part of that confusion is to establish which were legal established measures, and what quantity in modern terms did they contain. At the Union of 1707 with the English, Scots measures were brought into line with those south of the Border, but they continued in use in Scotland for at least a century longer. The table of measures in use in Scottish taverns and inns was:

4 gills	1 mutchkin
2 mutchkins	1 chopin
2 chopins	1 pint

The relation of these to English measures was as follows:

Scots	English
1 gill	$\frac{4}{5}$ gill
1 mutchkin	3 gills
1 chopin	1 pint and two gills
1 pint (the famous Tappit Hen)	3 pints
1 gallon	3 gallons

The Tappit Hen, then, which was plied so fervently in the taverns and dining halls, contained three pints English or sixty fluid ounces. The derivation of the word may be from the French quart measure 'toypnett'. Be that as it may, it was known in Scotland in the sixteenth century when French influence was strong.

There were other containers in use for drinking, although the 'bicker' was the common one. This was a bowl-shaped wooden vessel usually with two lugs or ears. A song to William Marshall, butler to the Duke of Gordon in the 1780s, and distinguished composer of Scottish melodies, mentions it:

> Butler, put around the claret
> Through us a' divide and share it,
> Gordon Castle weel can spare it
>   It has claret plenty;
> Wine's the true inspiring liquor,
> Draffy drink may please the vicar
> When he grasps the foaming bicker –
>   Vicars are not dainty.

To drink beer from it seems to have been its proper function. John Ramsay of Ochtertyre speaks of it being used in what he seems to regard as an improper function when he describes a confused inspection of the Monteith Volunteers in March 1804. 'They at last got too much whisky, drinking it out of bickers, which produced rioting.' (*Scottish Historical Publications*, Edinburgh, 1966, ed. Barbara Horn, p. 116.)

The word 'quaich' is from the Gaelic *cuach*, a bowl; these were frequently made and used throughout the country, not only in the Highlands. They were generally made of wooden staves bound together with hoops of metal, usually silver. The Gaelic *stòp*, a jug or flagon, is also found as 'stoup'. This was a wooden vessel which stood about eighteen inches in height, although the word was also used in conjunction with a specific measure, such as *stòp-mùisgin*, 'mutchkin-stoup'.

The cogue, cogie, coggie or cog was a widely used vessel, again with no fixed capacity or function. Burns uses the word frequently. In one of his finest verses he describes his coggie as a holy pool:

My coggie is a haly pool
That heals the wounds o' care and dool;
And Pleasure is a wanton trout,
And ye drink but deep ye'll find him out.

Burns also mentions these lines associated with the folksong
'Cauld Kale' in Aberdeen as being old in his time:

Yet here's to ilka honest soul
Wha'll drink wi' me a cogie;
And for ilka silly whinging fool,
We'll dook him in a bogie.

For I maun hae' my cogie sirs,
I canna want my cogie;
I wadna gie my thrie-gir'd cog
For a' the queans in Bogie.

Despite a little light such as this on drinking vessels we can
never be sure just what a man means in the eighteenth century
when he says he has drunk a pint of liquor, whether an English
pint or, in fact, three English pints, unless he specifies the
nationality of his measure. We know that Duncan Forbes was
fond of his Tappit Hens but when he says he drank five pints
of wine with the Provost of Elgin we cannot be sure whether
he has slipped into the English mode momentarily. As to the
impossible Lady Bridekirk, Alexander Carlyle makes it quite
clear that the pint bottle of brandy she was so fond of quaffing
was indeed a Scots pint.

Notes to chapter

[1] Preference for dark rum is still noticeable in some parts of Scotland, particularly in areas bordering the Highlands, such as the coastal districts in the east and parts of Perthshire.

[2] Temporarily one-handed.

4

Bad Laws and the Illicit Still

Despite the troubles following the imposition of the Malt Tax, Scotland, in terms of revenue legislation, had on the whole, a better time of it than England. The repressive measures taken in England to combat the social malady of the 'gin age' were not applied to Scotland. Even in the more enlightened Act of 1743 there was a clause exempting Scotland.

Perhaps the most famous of the privileges enjoyed in Scotland was 'Forbes' chartered boast'. In the year 1689, the estate of the anti-Jacobite Forbes of Culloden was ravaged by a body of some 700 'Highland rebels', while Forbes himself was absent in Holland. The losses incurred included 'his ancient brewary of aquavity'. The following year in settlement of his claim to compensation of about £4,500 sterling, the Scots Parliament granted him and his descendants the right to distil whisky from grain grown on their own property, free of duty.

At Edinburgh, 22nd July, 1690.
Our Sovereign Lord and Ladye, the King and Queen's Majesties and the three Estates of Parliament: Considering that the lands of Ferintosh were an ancient Brewary of Aquavity; and were still in use to pay a considerable Excise to the Treasury, while of late they were laid waste of the King's enemies; and it being just to give such as have suffered all possible encouragement, and also necessary to use all law-

58

ful endeavours for upholding of the King's Revenue: Therefore their Majesties and the Estates of Parliament for encouragement to the possessors of the said Lands to set up again
and prosecute their former trade of brewing and pay a duty
of Excyse as formerly; do hereby Ferm for the time to come
the yearly Excyse of the said lands of Ferintosh to the
present Duncan Forbes of Culloden, and his Successors,
Heritors of the same for the sum of 400 merks Scots. . . .

While the Act mentions a yearly duty of Excise it cannot be
interpreted as meaning just that. In 'farming' the duty to
Forbes for a small annual sum of about £22, taking into account
that the arable land on the Forbes estate extended to about
1,800 acres, we can see what a valuable gift he obtained. At the
same time any grain imported into the Culloden estate for
food or sowing did not come under Excise duty. This meant
that the entire produce of his considerable area of arable land
could be converted into whisky. Indeed there seem to have
been at least four distilleries on the Ferintosh estate and it has
been estimated that it produced more than all the rest of
Scotland. Forbes' profit has been estimated at about £18,000
per annum. Naturally such privileges aroused resentment
among other distillers and questions were asked in Parliament.
Among other things it was stated that his immunity wronged
his neighbours, that he had a virtual monopoly of distilling
and that his loss in the Jacobite raid was not above a year's
rent.

But Forbes and, indeed, the whole of the industry in Scotland
were not going to get away with it. The Government in London
saw the possibility of a rich harvest in the distilleries of Scotland.
They were also subjected to the influence of pressure groups of
English distillers who were angry at the increasing amount of
under-priced whisky that was flooding over the Border and
who did not bother to consider whether its popularity was due
to cheapness or its greater palatability. It is interesting to see

that Lord President Duncan Forbes was troubled by the small-
ness of the revenues of his day.

> The imminent distress, from the condition of our Revenue,
> has now for some time possessed my attention; the Customs,
> from the defects of the law, from the corruption of officers,
> and from the perverseness of juries, are fallen to nothing;
> and never can by any art be raised, till those complaints
> are removed, which must be the work of some time, though
> our disease seems to demand a more speedy remedy.
>
> The Excise, though not under so correct management
> as formerly, seems to be the only revenue from which we
> can look for any immediate relief, but unless it is put on a
> better foot, we cannot depend upon its answering any
> immediate purpose.
>
> (*Culloden Papers*, quoted from Menary)

But it did not occur to him that to give up his own privileges
might increase the yield of the Excise. He concluded that the
large quantities of foreign uncustomed brandy were the chief
cause of the poorness of revenue. At a Convention of Royal
burghs in 1730 he managed to get approval of a resolution
against the drinking of all foreign spirits. The idea was that all
burghs and counties should put such resolutions into effect and
abandon the use of foreign spirits after a certain date. Indeed,
they were to exert themselves to seize and destroy them whenever possible. But although the county of Midlothian did
actually execute such a resolution, he met with little success
elsewhere. The laws against what he calls 'that pernicious drug'
– uncustomed brandy – were not being enforced properly.

About this time he had other plans for raising the revenue,
such as leather duty and candle duty, but it was not until he
compiled his Memorial describing the revenues and manu-
factures of Scotland in 1742, that he set out his plans in detail.
By this time a new element has entered the picture. The main
cause of the low returns he finds is the excessive use by all

classes of the new drug tea. Even the labouring classes drink it for breakfast instead of the traditional ale. At this time the Ostend and Gottenburg Companies were importing large quantities of it into northern Europe and from there it was easily smuggled into Scotland. Women of the lower classes, in Forbes' view, took to imitating their betters and because 'run' tea could be had in Scotland for as little as 2s. 6d. per pound, they drank it to the exclusion of twopenny ale. He gives a number of remedies for this state of affairs. Put a tax of four shillings per pound on all tea imported, at the same time putting an end to smuggling, and the situation will right itself. Also tea should be forbidden to those who could not afford it at that duty. For instance, all servants should be forbidden the use of tea, but if it should be injurious to their health to forgo it, they could continue to drink it on the payment of an annual licence. The importation of foreign spirits is again mentioned, but it is now very much a secondary problem to Forbes compared with that of tea.

Perhaps it would be unfair to impute to Forbes the motive of distracting attention from the duty-free whisky of Ferintosh or to further its sale. Certainly he has little to say about whisky but as regards tea we must remember that many people of his time and later were very apprehensive of the effects of the new habit. Some thought strong tea drunk black was destructive to the nervous system, and while some people thought that the injurious effects of tea could be corrected by the addition of a little whisky, there were others, such as Hugo Arnott, who condemned both. In his *History of Edinburgh*, he says: 'Instead of malt liquor [i.e. ale] the lower class of people have betaken themselves to tea and whisky. The first of these, to people who are not able to afford generous diet and liquors, cannot be esteemed wholesome. The last is equally pernicious to health and morals.'

Although Lord President Forbes died a good many years before Arnott wrote his history, we can imagine him disagreeing heartily with what the latter had to say about whisky. In a footnote on the same page (p. 335) he continues:

It is needless to descant upon the tendency of this evil. It is so important a nature as to require the hand of government to root it out, before the pernicious habit of the capital spreads itself over the country. Besides the licensed stills which are only eight in number, it is computed that there are in Edinburgh no fewer than four hundred private stills which pay no duty to the government, but distil in private the poison which is afterwards retailed among the inhabitants. This estimate is, however, only conjecture. The following is certain. Dr. Percival expressed his regret that there are in Manchester (pop. 43,000) no fewer than 193 licensed houses for retailing spirituous liquors. How much more would the Doctor have had occasion to express his concern in the county of Edinburgh, a district which does not contain 100,000 people, yet in which there are 2,000 houses which retail spirituous and other liquors.

Arnott made up his figures as follows:

Houses licensed by magistrates	1,611
No. of annual convictions for illicit retail	200
No. supposed to escape	200
Total	2,011

Arnott, after the manner of Forbes with tea, shows a strain of patriarchal tyranny when he proposes that every means be used to lessen the production of whisky. He advocates a lesser tax on ale and a higher tax on whisky. He points out that only 159 of the 1,611 licensed houses in Edinburgh applied for licences to retail foreign spirits, the remaining 1,452 being 'destined for the entertainment of the lower class of people'. He believes that if ale and beer were available at a moderate price, it would never be in the interest of government or humanity 'that spirituous liquors should be at the command of the indigent'.

There were blasts on the same theme also from the pages of the *Older Statistical Account*. The Reverend George Home says:

Tradesmen and labourers are addicted to the pernicious habit of using tea. Of late also, from the low price of whisky, the execrable custom of *dram drinking* is gaining ground, even among the women of the lower class. Habits so inimical to health, industry and morals ought to be checked if possible. . . .

Despite all he says, he adds, 'They seem contented with their situation and are not strangers to the comforts of life.'

During the second quarter of the eighteenth century, whisky had been becoming more popular in the Lowlands, coinciding with the fall of the production of twopenny ale. This probably began after the imposition of the Malt Tax in 1725 when home brewing began to decline. The drink of the lower classes was almost entirely twopenny, but about 1750 they turned more and more to whisky. Tobias Smollett, in J. Melford's letter from Argyleshire in *Humphrey Clinker*, comments on the varying drinking habits of Lowlander and Highlander:

When the Lowlanders want to drink a chearupping-cup, they go to the public house which they call a Change-house, and call for a chopine of twopenny, which is a thin, yeasty beverage, made of malt; not quite so strong as the table-beer of England. This is brought in a pewter stoop shaped like a skittle, from whence it is emptied into a quaff;[1] that is, a curious cup made of different pieces of wood, such as box and ebony, cut into little staves, jointed alternately, and secured with delicate hoops, having two ears or handles. It holds about a gill, is sometimes tipt about the mouth with silver, and has a plate of the same metal at bottom, with the landlord's cypher engraved. The

Highlanders on the other hand, regale themselves with whisky; a malt spirit as strong as geneva, which they swallow in great quantities without any signs of inebriation. They are used to it from the cradle, and find it an excellent preservative against the winter cold, which must be extreme on these mountains. I am told that it is given with great success to infants, as a cordial in the confluent smallpox when the eruption seems to flag, and the symptoms grow unfavourable. The Highlanders eat more animal food than falls to the share of their neighbours in the Low-country. They delight in the chase. . . .

In this passage Smollett seems to realize the profound suitability of whisky, and particularly malt whisky, to an open-air life. It is at its best after a tramp on a rocky shore or a windy hill.

Funerals and weddings were the chief occasions for mass drinking. Five glasses were normally drunk before a funeral party set out, and it was not unknown for them to lose the coffin on the way. Smollett tells of the funeral he attended in Argyleshire:

Yesterday we were invited to the funeral of an old lady, the grand-mother of a gentleman in this neighbourhood, and found ourselves in the midst of fifty people, who were regaled with a sumptuous feast, accompanied by the music of a dozen pipers. In short, this meeting had all the air of a grand festival; and the guests did such honour to the entertainment, that many of them could not stand when reminded of the business on which we had met. The company forthwith taking horse, rode in a very irregular cavalcade to the place of interment, a church, at the distance of two long miles from the castle. On our arrival, however, we found that we had committed a small oversight, in leaving the corpse behind; so that we were obliged to wheel about, and met the old woman half way, carried upon poles by the nearest relations of her family, and attended by the *coronach*, composed of a multitude of old hags, who tore their hair, beat their breasts, and howled most hideously. At the grave, the orator, or the *senachie*, pronounced the panegyric of the defunct, every period being confirmed by a yell of the *coronach*. The body was committed to the earth, the pipers playing a pibroch all the time; and all the company standing uncovered. The ceremony was closed with a discharge of pistols; then we returned to the castle, resumed the bottle, and by midnight there was not a sober person in the family, the females excepted. The squire and I were, with some difficulty permitted to retire with our landlord in the evening; but our entertainer was a little chagrined at our retreat, and afterwards seemed to think it a disparagement to his family, that not above a hundred gallons of whisky had been drank on such a solemn occasion. This morning we got up by four to hunt the roebuck. . . .

This is not merely a story about incidents which happened and could only happen in the mid-eighteenth century. Within living memory, at the funeral of an old lady on a certain island in the Outer Hebrides, the rather high-spirited company set off with the empty coffin, commenting to each other that Margaret must have wasted away a lot during her last illness. They buried the coffin with all ceremony and returned to the house of mourning to find old Margaret's body still stretched out and awaiting burial. At the funeral of Fraser of Lovat in 1815, it is said that some of the mourners drank so much that they fell into the vault.

In any case, to return to the spread of the habit of drinking whisky into the Lowlands and into England and to the desire of the Government to tap such a rich source of revenue, they went ahead with legislation and with plans to change the methods of collecting revenue. Collection was difficult or impracticable in remote districts and it was stated that the revenue from distilling should be much greater than it actually was. The Government decided to develop a licence system based on the quantity of the wash that could be used by a still, and presumed that a given quantity must yield a given percentage of spirit. This took no account of the *gravity* of the wash. No account was taken of the crude high gravity and artificially saccharified wash that was commonly used by the English distillers, and the weak natural wash used in Scotland. In Scotland, the product of the still was for consumption without adulteration or artificial flavouring of any kind, whereas in England the distiller produced a coarse spirit for rectification, a further distilling mixed with various essences. This was one of the reasons for the rise of illicit distilling almost to the status of an industry. The authorities thought that they knew all about the science of distilling and by charging a licence based on the wash content of a still they could not only compute the precise quantity of the distilled spirit, but they could save a great deal of expense by not having to supervise licensed distilleries perpetually. The outcome of this illogical thought was the Wash Act of 1784. It did not succeed and was superseded in 1786 by an Act which did not press the ratio between wash and spirit and concentrated on licence.

The Act, besides favouring the English distillers in its specifications, made one fundamental mistake. It assumed that a still could not be worked off in less than twenty-four hours. The distillers soon spotted this assumption and they began to devise means for increasing the output of their stills without altering their capacity. The Act of 1786 said nothing about quantity of output except in relation to a still's content and the assumed time it took to work it off. A still could be any shape, and it was not long before exotically shaped stills made their appearance. These vessels reduced further and further the time of working off. The Government was caught on one foot, and desperately increased the duty at successive intervals. The licence that had been fixed at £1 10s. in 1786 was £3 by 1788. The race between the distillers and the revenue authorities was on. By 1793 it was £9 and in 1797 it was £54. By 1803 it was at the height of £163, and it was said that some of the new stills could be worked off in about three minutes. So much for the Government's lack of foresight and the ingenuity of the Scots distiller. It can easily be appreciated, however, that the people who were gaining were the distillers who could afford, almost continuously, to build new stills to keep ahead of the legislation. The situation was very difficult for the smaller men and they had the choice between being driven out of business or of going into illicit production.

The licence system had been extended to the Highlands in 1787, with a rate of twenty shillings per gallon of still content as opposed to the Lowland rate of thirty shillings. It is not quite clear why this distinction was made. There were many arguments, some of them true enough and some others false. In this respect I quote from the book *Scotch Made Easy* by Ross Wilson:

> The arguments in favour of the distinction between the Highlands and Lowlands were many. It diminished, it was thought, the incentive of illicit distillation in remote parts; grain in the Highlands was considered of an inferior quality which would result in less spirit being yielded; the harvests in the north were thought more precarious; and the Highland distiller was justifiably considered to be inferior to his Lowland brother in capital. Rather more doubtfully, the Highland still was thought inferior in itself; it may have been in the amount of spirit yielded over a given period, but certainly not in the quality of the spirit – anything but.

To people with a knowledge of the country it is interesting to see the boundary between Highland and Lowland defined by Act of Parliament.

A certain line or boundary beginning at the east point of Loch Crinan, and proceeding from thence to Loch Gilpin; from thence along the great road along the west side of Loch Fyne, to Inveraray and to the head of Loch Fyne; from thence along the high road to Arrochar, in the county of Dunbarton, and from thence to Tarbet; from Tarbet in a supposed line straight eastward on the north side of the mountain called Ben Lomond, to the village of Callander of Monteith in the county of Perth; from thence north eastward to Crieff; from thence northward to Ambleree and Inver to Dunkeld; from thence along the foot and south side of the Grampian Hills to Fettercairn, in the county of Kincardine; and from thence northward along the road to Cuttie's Hillock, Kincardine O'Neil, Clatt, Huntly, and Keith to Fochabers; and from thence westward by Elgin and Forres, to the boat on the River Findhorn, and from thence down the said river to the sea at Findhorn, and any place in or part of the county of Elgin, which lies southward of the said line from Fochabers to the sea at Findhorn.

Illicit distilling continued and increased almost to the status of an industry, in both the Highland zone and in the Lowland.

Among the actions which must also have increased smuggling activities was the removal by the Government of 'Forbes' chartered boast' referred to above. For many years, indeed since the establishment of a Board of Excise in 1707, the Treasury had been pressed to buy this right. It certainly was an anomaly in an age of increasing duty and caused dissatisfaction among other distillers everywhere. The Government acted ultimately in 1784, the year of the infamous Wash Act and the year of the beginning of troubled times in the whisky industry. An Act was passed to arrange the takeover:

Whereas Arthur Forbes of Culloden Esq., in the county of Inverness, is possessed of an exemption from the duties of Excise, within the lands of Ferintosh, under several Acts of

Parliament of Scotland, which exemption has been found detrimental to the revenue and to the distillery in other parts of Scotland enacted that the Treasury shall agree with the said Arthur Forbes upon a compensation to be paid to him in lieu of the exemption and if they shall not agree, the Barons of Exchequer may settle the compensation by a jury, and after payment thereof, the said exemption shall cease.

In that year the Government paid £21,000 to Forbes and the exemption did cease. Thus was ended the great Ferintosh whisky of the eighteenth century, revered by Gaelic poets and Robert Burns alike.

It may have brought a little peace to the industry in Scotland if it had not come with unsavoury legislation. Certainly it appeared to bring some peace to the Highland town of Dingwall according to *The Domestic Annals of Scotland*. The minister of the town, in his account of the parish, talking a few years after the abolition of exemption tells that during the period of the privilege there were many quarrels and breaches of the peace among the inhabitants and these yielded a good harvest of business among the lawyers of Dingwall. But after exemption the people became more peaceful towards each other and the legal profession declined. I take this reference from an article by Ian MacDonald in *Transactions of the Gaelic Society of Inverness*, vol. XII.

To return to the onward rush of legislation. In 1798 there came another Act, this time retaining the still licence, but also increasing the duty on the actual spirit. This imposed a further sixpence on each gallon of spirits imported into England and caused distress to many Scotch distillers. Among those to close down were John and James Stein at Kennetpans and Kilbagie, both near Alloa, and John and James Haig of Canonmills, Edinburgh. Sir William Forbes of Pitsligo was then head of a banking house in Edinburgh and in his *Memoirs of a Banking*

House, had something to say about their fall. The Stein brothers were the biggest malt distillers in Scotland and used Forbes' bank (later to be merged with the Union Bank of Scotland) for considerable credit facilities. He says of them: 'not content with the sale of spirits in Scotland, they resolved to rival the distilleries of London by manufacturing spirits for the English market, which they conceived themselves enabled to do by some advantage in their situation in Scotland'.

Of their actual fall, Forbes says: 'For a considerable time they had been carrying on a losing trade in a foolish and fruitless contest with distillers, who, being a great and opulent body of men, had kept down the price of spirits in order to drive their Scotch competitors out of the market – a proof of which was their largely raising the price immediately on those bankruptcies taking place. This contest with the London distillers they had only been enabled to support by their circulation of bills in London. . . .'

In 1799 the Scotch distillers were in a really bad way. In February of that year they presented a petition, consisting of some 550 words, to the House of Commons. While they praise the distillery Licence Act of 1786, 'hawking and smuggling have been annihilated, Spirit Dealers have been left in the pursuit of an honest profession', they regretfully take the liberty of complaining about a recent addition of a shilling per gallon tax on spirits, in addition to the licence duty. They complain that they are going to be priced out of the market once again: 'Hawkers and smugglers have returned to their former occupations, and thus are the natural customers of the Petitioners supplied with spirits from the old sources, to the ruin of the Petitioners.' They were justified in their fears. The smugglers were certainly prospering as never before, and their prosperity was due to legislation which, in fact, prevented licensed distillers making good whisky.

The wrong type of legislation reached its peak in 1814, when the whole licence system based on the size of the still was thrown away. The Government reverted to a system based on duties on the wash and on the spirit, with a licence of ten pounds for the privilege of distilling. We have mentioned the unfairness of the original Wash Act in not taking into account the difference between the gravity of the wash used in England and that used in Scotland. This was now corrected by an instrument known as the saccharimeter. This could measure the gravity of any given wash, and duty was paid accordingly. This naturally removed any tendency on the part of the distiller to prepare a wash as strong as possible in order to get as much spirit as he could. While the saccharimeter removed one injustice, the Government, however, added another one. It prohibited stills of less than five hundred gallons capacity.

Colonel Stewart of Garth speaks of the iniquity of this Act with respect to the Highland area:

It is evident that this law was a complete interdict, as a still of this magnitude would consume more than the disposable grain in the most extensive county within this newly drawn boundary; nor could fuel be obtained for such an establishment without an expense which the commodity could not possibly bear. The sale, too, of the spirits produced was circumscribed within the same line,* and thus the market which alone could have supported the manufacture was entirely cut off. Although the quantity of grain raised within many districts, in consequence of the recent agricultural improvements, greatly exceeds the consumption, the inferior quality of this grain, and the great expense of carrying it to the Lowland distillers, who, by a ready market, and the command of fuel, can more easily accommodate themselves to this law, renders it impracticable for the farmers to dispose of their grain in any manner adequate to pay rents equal to the real value of their farms,

* In consequence of an action brought by the Lowland distillers in 1814 against the Board of Excise, Highland distillers were not allowed to market their spirits south of the Grampians.

subject as they are to the many drawbacks of uncertain climate, uneven surface, distance from market, and scarcity of fuel. Thus hardly any alternative remained but that of having recourse to illicit distillation, or resignation of their farms and breach of their engagements with their landlords. These are difficulties of which the Highlanders complain heavily, asserting that nature and the distillery laws present unsurmountable obstacles to the carrying on of a legal traffic. The surplus produce of their agricultural labour will therefore remain on their hands, unless they incur an expense beyond what that article will bear, in conveying so bulky a commodity to the Lowland market as the raw material, and the drawback of prices on their inferior grain. In this manner, their produce must be disposed of at a great loss, as it cannot be legally manufactured in the country. Hence they resort to smuggling as their only resource. If it indeed be true that this illegal traffic has made such deplorable breaches in the honesty and morals of the people, the revenue drawn from the large distilleries, to which the Highlanders have been made the sacrifice, has been procured at too high a price for the country.

Stewart of Garth knew his Highlands very well, with their necessities and their difficulties. Not so, many travellers who wrote memoirs of their Highland journeys. Allan Cunningham said that he never heard Sir Walter Scott mention Leyden but with 'an expression of regard and a moistening of the eye'.

The rather unobservant Dr. John Leyden travelled the Highlands in the year 1800 and thoroughly disapproved of the illicit distillation of whisky.

The distillation of whiskey presents an irresistible temptation to the poorer classes, as the boll of barley, which costs thirty shillings, produces by this process, between five and six guineas. This distillation had a most ruinous effect in increasing the scarcity of grain last year, particularly in

Isla and Tiree, where the people subsisted chiefly on fish and potatoes.

(Journal of a Tour to the Highlands in 1800, John Leyden, Edinburgh, 1803, p. 79)

Dr. Leyden does not seem to have been a very good economist. Converting thirty shillings into five guineas would appear to be good business. One wonders if Leyden ever met the minister of Killearnan in Ross-shire who wrote in the *Old Statistical Account*: 'Distilling is almost the only method of converting our victual into cash for the payment of rent and servants, and whisky, may, in fact, be called our staple commodity.' (*O.S.A.* xvii, 352.)

But Leyden was not altogether without humour in his observations of the effect their own native product had on the native Highlanders which he encountered. In the same volume he describes his journey in a chaise from Oban to Bunawe: 'Our driver, in order to elevate his spirits before setting out on the dreary road, had applied himself to whisky, the universal medicine of the Highlanders, and not being extremely accurate in his calculations, had raised them considerably over par, and therefore amused himself by dismounting every gate which he encountered and hurling them over the braes or into Loch Etive.'

To return to the subject of illicit distillation, or smuggling. We must remember that in the eighteenth and nineteenth centuries these words were virtually synonymous. The illicit distiller was invariably called a smuggler as were those who were found to be in possession of uncustomed spirits.

Whisky was undoubtedly being distilled in the Highlands long before the furore about new legislation raised itself. The earlier stills, apart from the complex of Ferintosh, would distil only for a family or perhaps a circle of friends or a small district. The situation changed when the restrictions on legal distillers made it difficult or impossible for them to continue

73

to make a livelihood out of it. Furthermore, the situation depicted above by Stewart of Garth, would bring pressure on the small distillers who perhaps brewed only occasionally, to expand their plant and to increase production. They were, in fact, entering into competition with legal producers. In the remote glens of the northern and central Highlands the illicit spirit was made, often in stills of a portable kind, and transported by various devious routes to the markets of the south. By contrast to Stewart of Garth's calm assessment of the nature of this problem, there were many who regarded it simply as a criminal activity. The Exciseman quoted above, Ian MacDonald, writing in the *Transactions of the Gaelic Society of Inverness*, says: 'It is difficult to conceive the terrible amount of lawlessness, of turbulence, of loss and injury connected with such matters, and cases are known where not only individuals but communities never recovered temporal prosperity after successful raids by the military, cutters, and gaugers'. Attempts were made during this period to establish legal distilleries within the Highland area, but as the law stood this was very difficult.

In his evidence before a Parliamentary Commission which sat from 1833 to 1836, Captain H. Munro of the Teaninich distillery in Ross-shire (which still exists) said that there was great concern in the county in the year 1817 about the injurious effects of illicit distilling. The proprietors passed resolutions to abolish smuggling and to encourage the erection of legal distilleries. He goes on:

Accordingly three or four were built, one in particular by several gentlemen combining, and the Teaninich distillery was built by me on my own property; yet it so happened that the illicit distillers commanded the grain market of the country, and the resolutions were not carried into effect; smuggling still existed and the success of the distilleries disappointed the expectations of those who carried them on.

74

The partnership of one was dissolved, with a loss of £500 to each proprietor concerned. Two others were soon given up. . . .

Undoubtedly there were many in positions of authority who condoned, if not actually encouraged, smuggling. Fransai Mor Mac an Aba, JP, Chief of the Clan MacNab, appears to have actively supported them. According to an article in Gaelic in the *Transactions of the Gaelic Society of Inverness*, vol. xxxiii, he particularly helped smugglers in the Callander and Loch Vennachar areas. On one occasion he was supposed to have procured a key for a smuggler to obtain access to his confiscated cask of whisky. The cask was exchanged for a cask of water. The case came up in court with MacNab himself on the bench. When the whisky was duly tested, the furious MacNab ordered the case to be dismissed and the unfortunate gauger to be charged with contempt of court. It was also said that on one occasion he refused either to join or sanction an expedition to intercept a smuggling convoy passing through Killin at night because the place was haunted with fairies and goblins. The same writer also tells of the notoriety of the smugglers of the Glen Quoich area for being their own best customers. Basins of wash were left lying around in the open frequently and the cattle became drunk. There were also two taverns, presumably unlicensed, in Glen Quoich, bearing the unlikely titles of 'Lower Cheapside' and 'Upper Cheapside'. The owner of one was a woman who served a dram with one hand while she held a Gaelic Psalm Book in the other, and an admonishment on her lips. The customers called her 'a witch with her eye on Heaven and her heart on earth'.

The book *Report of the Trial of Malcolm Gillespie for Forgery*, published in Aberdeen in 1827, gives an interesting account of the patronage of smugglers by people in authority. Gillespie was a well-known Revenue officer in the north-east of Scotland during the first quarter of the eighteenth century, and this book also gives an account of some of his exploits as a hard and daring gauger.

A notorious smuggler by the name of Grant, accompanied by his two sons, used to run whisky into Stonehaven. Gillespie met this 'banditti' on their way into town one night with a horse and cart loaded with contraband whisky. After a severe fight he managed to seize the horse and cart and some of the whisky. The elder Grant then said to him that the whisky was for a certain Justice of the Peace in the town, and that he, Gillespie, would be removed from his post if the whisky was seized. When the case came up two days later, the same JP was on the bench and while he confiscated the whisky, he ordered the horse and cart to be returned to their owners, the accused. To cap it all, he proceeded to find the Excise liable in the expenses of the case.

Sillett in his book *Illicit Scotch* quotes a glowing example of an 'involved magistrate' in Tain. His name was William Murray and he combined the duties of a bank agent with those of estate factor, merchant and Justice of the Peace. The smugglers bought their barley and other goods from him, and in return, enjoyed his protection in court. Both magistrates and lawyers accepted presents of contraband whisky for their services, and it is said that a woman from Campbeltown testified to the sheriff that 'I haena made a drop since yon wee keg I sent to yoursel'.'

There were also some gaugers who accepted bribes, usually in the form of a percentage of the duty that would have been charged on the whisky had it been legal. Their wives also benefited by giving information to the smugglers about the movements of Riding Officers in the neighbourhood.

The smugglers could grow very bold and it was not unknown for Excise officers to be shown a still at work and coolly defied to make a seizure. The man who could defy the gauger was a hero in his own circle and the first decade of the nineteenth century was indeed the 'heroic age' of whisky. Pitched battles between the smugglers and the gaugers were not unknown, such as that at Sliabh Choire Mhuc Locha in Perthshire between men from Atholl and Excisemen supported by mounted troops. The smugglers in this case fought off the troops and saved the whisky. An account of this incident is given in the Gaelic paper quoted above, and was taken from one of the smugglers concerned. He spent twenty years in France after the affair and died in Perthshire in about 1896.

The violence of a gauger's life in or on the fringes of the Highlands in those times is well illustrated in the account of Malcolm Gillespie's life in the book quoted above. Perhaps Gillespie was the first of his office to train a dog for his detection work. He trained a bull-terrier to seize horses by the nose and make them rear up and drop their loads. The first engagement using the dog took place at Midmar Lodge in Aberdeenshire on 8 February 1816, when a party of smugglers was discovered with four horses laden with whisky. A 'desperate struggle' between the smugglers and Gillespie and his assistants took place, and the dog played his part well by seizing each horse in turn by the nose until all the ankers of whisky were thrown from their backs. Four of these ankers were staved and Gillespie seized the remaining four. Gillespie and his dog had another memorable engagement on 30 July of the same year. He detected a group of eight Highlanders with four laden horses approaching Kintore. They were led by a man called MacHardy, and in other areas they had already deforced all the Revenue officers who had attempted to stop them. Indeed, some of them were already outlawed. Gillespie shot one of their horses dead with his pistol, but when he cornered the others in an avenue with their backs to a large iron gate, they shot dead his redoubtable bull-terrier. When reinforcements came up, however, the smugglers surrendered without further loss of life. The 'banditti' in this case had bludgeons and firearms, and the fore-ends of their carts were stocked with large quantities of stones 'of a size suitable for an engagement'.

Gillespie's most desperate encounter, and in which he received permanent injuries, was with a group of Highlanders on their way to Aberdeen with whisky on 30 December 1818. His sabre was taken from him in the struggle and he received a deep wound in the face. However, when he wounded one of the smugglers with his pistol and called on his assistants to put white belts on like the military, and to fire together, the enemy retired. Gillespie had internal injuries as well as surface wounds.

He was executed in Aberdeen on 16 November 1827, after being convicted of forgery, an offence not connected with his work as an Exciseman. In his dying statement, he said that he had over forty wounds on his body to show for his work in the service of the Government.

Other Excise officers were also very zealous in carrying out their duties. Sillett records that in the space of six years, the officer on the Clatt Ride effected a total of 1,217 detections, many of them in very difficult circumstances. In October 1815, one Duncan MacPherson of Auchindoir took such violent exception to the seizure of two casks of whisky and some wash, that, in the officer's own words, 'he threatened me with immediate death if I offered to destroy any more, at the same time beating and bruising me to the effusion of blood, so far as medical aid was necessary'.

Other gaugers were also deforced and pursued by angry smugglers who saw them as foreign interlopers bent on destroying the only means of livelihood that they had. In October 1817 George Arthur, Supervisor of Excise, was killed in a skirmish near Campbeltown. Two men were arrested and tried for murder and acquitted for lack of evidence. Another gauger in the Cabrach was shot dead by a bullet which was said to have been intended for his horse. It was widely believed in the area that it was fired by a schoolteacher called Robertson. The police arrested a local farm servant, Adam Gordon, and he was tried for murder. He made no statement whatsoever during the three-day hearing at Aberdeen and the Judge ordered his release.

On the other hand, a number of gaugers were tried for the murder of smugglers and this may explain how loath they were on many occasions to use their firearms.

It cannot be too strongly emphasized that smuggling on any considerable scale in the Highlands came into being through necessity. It began at a time when the Government threatened to strangle the community by unsympathetic laws. As such it was a brief phase in time and was ended not by the ever-increasing force of Excisemen and their helpers, but by new legislation.

As to the quick growth of smuggling we may refer again to Colonel Stewart of Garth. He published his book *Sketches of the Highlanders of Scotland* in 1822 when smuggling was reaching its peak. Stewart speaks of its growth:

> So little was it practised in the Perthshire Highlands that a tenant of my grandfather's was distinguished by the appellation of 'Donald Whisky', from his being a distiller and smuggler of that spirit. If all existing were to be named from this traffic, five of the most numerous clans of the country conjoined could not produce so many of one name. In the year 1778, there was only one officer of Excise in that part of Perthshire above Dunkeld, and he had little employment. In the same district, there are now eleven resident officers in full activity, besides Rangers (as they are called) and extra officers sent to see that the resident officers are doing their duty; yet, so rapidly did illicit distillation increase, that it would seem as if the greater the number of officers appointed, the more employment they found for themselves; and it is a common, and, I believe, a just remark, that whenever an officer is placed in a glen, he is not long without business.

Stewart considers the year 1786, when the Pitt government

79

checked the importation of foreign spirits, as an important year in the development of illicit distilling. He says that brandy and rum landed on the west coast was the principal 'spirituous drink' of the inhabitants. He also regards the recent land improvements as a cause, but more important was the legislation that made good legal whisky almost impossible to produce, and the undoubted fact that everybody preferred smuggled whisky. It is claimed that King George IV liked smuggled Glenlivet. In his book *A Hundred Years in the Highlands*, Osgood MacKenzie recalls his father's preference for it:

> In my father's day and long after it, doctors and every other person were satisfied that health depended greatly on the quantity of 'good' liquor that a person swallowed daily. . . .
>
> I heard him say once, going unexpectedly to Gairloch without sending notice beforehand, he was surprised by the want of usual joy on his appearing, and was sure something was wrong. It turned out that a vessel loaded with brandy, claret etc. had been chased into the bay by a revenue cutter, and willing hands had carried the cargo into Tigh Dige into which my father had to enter by a ladder. . . . My father never tasted anything but smuggled whisky and when every mortal that called for him – they were legion daily – had a dram poured into him, the ankers of whisky emptied yearly must have been numerous indeed.

The townspeople were also busy distilling. We hear of the still that was found in the cellars under the Tron Kirk in the High Street of Edinburgh, but perhaps best of all was the still that operated in one of the hollow arches of the South Bridge in Edinburgh. A number of the arches of this bridge are blocked up by houses which line it on both sides, and it was in one of these that the distillery was found in 1815 after it had been working for eighteen months. The water supply had been obtained by tapping one of the mains of the water company which just passed overhead, the smoke was got rid of by boring a hole in the chimney of the neighbouring house, and the waste matter was disposed of by a communication with the soil pipes. The spirits were sent out to customers in tin cans of two or three gallons each, carried by a woman.

Most of the stories of smuggling, however, come from the Highlands. Many with the same theme are found in different localities. A typical one of these is as follows. The gaugers had seized a cask of whisky and carried it to an inn. They took it with them into the room in which they were taking refreshments. The smugglers bribed a servant girl to tell them the precise position of the cask. They then bored a hole in the floor directly underneath and emptied the contents of the confiscated cask into another one. The story is told in Mull and is also claimed for Bogroy Inn in Ross-shire. Another incident ended fatally at this same inn. After a brush with smugglers in Strathglass, a group of gaugers retired to Bogroy where one of them died of his injuries.

Ian MacDonald tells a good story about a smuggler called John Dearg. The character seems to be real since MacDonald, a gauger himself, describes him as being without any pretensions to piety and representing the clever, unscrupulous class of smugglers who frequently succeeded in outwitting the gaugers. He was successful in his craft and reputed to have acquired wealth by it. He was a kind of middleman as well as being a distiller himself. Once he had a large quantity of whisky in his house awaiting transport to Invergordon and word came that Excise officers were searching the neighbourhood. John knew that his house would have priority, and he asked a tailor who was in the habit of working from house to house and who was in his home at the time, to allow himself to be laid out as a corpse on the table, with a boll of malt as reward. The tailor agreed; a linen sheet was laid over him and a plate of salt was laid on his stomach while the women set up a lament and John

Dearg seized a Bible and turned up a suitable psalm. There was a loud knock at the door and the 'dead' tailor said to John Dearg, 'I will call out unless you give me two bolls.' The smuggler was outwitted perhaps for the first time in his life. The gaugers retreated embarrassed from the house of mourning and when they asked later when John Dearg's brother died, they were told that John Dearg never had a brother.

Many of the smugglers' activities, in twentieth-century terms, had much in common with the activities of a Resistance movement. The armed Excisemen, or gaugers, with their 'wicked iron-pointed sticks' poked on unenclosed ground everywhere and where any distilling equipment might be hidden. Even the peat stacks were not immune, for the gaugers well knew that a well-made stack could hide a valuable copper still. Their activities, as one writer put it, 'ended all peace and comfort in smuggling'.

Measures had to be taken to combat the gaugers' activities. The tales of defiance are legion, and vary from accounts of head-on armed conflicts on the highways to accounts of exquisite camouflage. The smugglers also resorted to age-old methods of alerting the population. No evidence as to the use of the Fiery Cross has survived, but they certainly used the well-tried method of lighting fires on prominent hills to warn anyone who felt that he might have a reason to feel enmity towards the Excisemen.

The whisky men of the mountains also knew how to recoup their losses. Students of Highland history will remember the progress of the disarmament campaigns of the first half of the eighteenth century. After attempting many times to make the Highland clans submit to the laws and customs of the country, the Government donned the velvet glove. They actually offered sums of money for arms surrendered to their garrisons in the Highlands at places such as Fort William, Fort Augustus and Fort George. A quick response came to this generous offer. There was no lack of broken or obsolete weapons in the untamed

Highlands of those days, and those not suitable for conflict were handed in to the rather naïve garrison officers in exchange for money. This money was useful in purchasing new weapons.

The Disarming Act of 1716 was well meant, as indeed was the later provision made for rewards to be given for the 'seizure' of a still. One of the most bizarre results of the former was to create a trade between Scotland and Holland in broken or obsolete weapons, and may even be said to have contributed to the more spectacular rebellion of 1745. One suspects also that the Disarming Act served as an inspiration to smugglers whose gear was becoming the worse for wear.

Robbie MacPherson of Glenrinnes and his confederates would appear to have been students of Highland history. They were not insensitive distillers like so many who dabbled in smuggling. They not only let their whisky get cold but they actually matured it, long before this practice became general. Assiduous workers require tools and the more assiduous the work the more frequently that tool will require to be replaced. When an important part of Robbie's distilling apparatus became sadly worn, he accepted a traditional solution as to the cost of replacement. A 'seizure' payment would be claimed. A special dummy bothy was constructed with all the clues that would lure the watchful gauger. When all was ready a member of the band was sent to report his 'find' to the Excisemen. He was immediately employed to keep a watch on the 'bothy' with one of the gaugers, and after a week of vigilant observation, he had raised the money for the necessary replacements.

There was a certain revival of smuggling in the 1880s. In his preface to the paper quoted on pp. 69 and 74, expanded into book form and published in 1914,[2] Ian MacDonald draws attention to this phenomenon:

For some time prior to 1880, illicit distillation had been practically suppressed in the north, and the old smugglers were fast passing away; but with the abolition of the Malt

83

Tax, the reduction of the Revenue Preventive Staff, and the feeling of independence produced by the Crofter's Act, came a violent and sustained outburst of smuggling which was not only serious as regards Revenue and licensed traders, but threatened to demoralise and impoverish the communities and districts affected. The revival among the youth of a new generation of those pernicious habits which had in the past led to so much lawlessness, dishonesty, idleness and drinking was especially lamentable.

While MacDonald condemns this later rise in distilling of this kind, he readily admits that while the still licence was in force in the Highlands from 1787 to 1814, and perhaps for some years later, the smugglers' whisky was undoubtedly superior in quality and flavour to that produced by the licensed distiller. But he claims that in the closing decades of the nineteenth century, this was no longer true:

The Highland distiller [i.e. legal] now has the best appliances, uses the best materials, employs skill and experience, exercises the greatest possible care, and further, matures his spirit in bond – whisky being highly deleterious unless it is matured by age. On the other hand, the smuggler uses rude, imperfect utensils, very often inferior materials, under every disadvantage and inconvenience, and is always in a state of terror and hurry, which is incompatible with good work and the best results. He begins by purchasing an inferior barley, which as a rule, is imperfectly malted. He brews without more idea of proper heats than dipping his finger or seeing his face in the water, and the quantity of the water is regulated by the size and the number of his vessels. His setting heat is decided by another dip of the finger, and supposing he has yeast of good quality, and may by accident add the proper quantity, the fermentation of his worts depends on the proper weather, as he cannot regulate the temperature in his temporary

84

bothy. . . . But the most fatal defect in the smuggler's appliances is the construction of his still. Ordinary stills have head elevations of from 12 to 18 feet, which serves for the purpose of rectification, as the fusel oils and other essential oils and acids fall back into the still, while the more alcoholic vapour, which is more volatile, passes over to the worm where it is condensed. The smuggler's still has no head elevation, the still-head being as flat as an old blue bonnet, and consequently, the essential oils and acids pass over with the alcohol into the worm, however carefully distillation is carried out.[3]

Perhaps MacDonald never heard of the dram called 'Kill the Cairter'. According to the *Scottish National Dictionary* this was a coarse whisky favoured by the Gilmerton carriers, a particularly rough class. Quote: 'He preferred his whisky to be strong and heady, with a suspicion of what he called "Fussle-ile" (fusel oil) in it – the variety of potation that is usually called "Kill the Cairter".'

While it is generally known that fusel oil is partly controlled by the height of the still-head, it is by no means certain that storing in wood eliminates these higher alcohols to any great extent from the whisky, as MacDonald claims in the context of the above quotation. But having sampled smuggled whisky in both the Highlands and in Ireland in recent years, I would tend to agree with him in his general assessment of its quality.

Since 1886, undoubtedly due to the work of active gaugers with high morals, like MacDonald himself, smuggling has been on the decline in the Highlands and is practically extinct. As he said, and we may believe him, 'I state frankly that the highest sense of duty would hardly sustain me in suppressing the smugglers on the West Coast, unless I also had a strong and deep conviction that if I could persuade or prevent them from engaging in smuggling, I should be doing them the greatest possible service.' His accounts of detections in this period of the revival of smuggling have the ring of truth about them. After lecturing a smuggler on his 'evil and dishonesty' once, the smuggler replied, 'The village merchant has kept my family and self alive for the last twelve months, and would you blame me if I made an effort to pay him something? There is no fishing and no work, and what am I to do?' Another said to him, 'If we are to be hunted like this, either get something for me to do or *cuir an gunna rium* – shoot me.' MacDonald admits that successful smuggling can be profitable in a 'pecuniary' sense. The year in which he wrote, 1885, the price of barley per quarter was 23s. Some fourteen to sixteen gallons of whisky could be obtained from this amount and would sell at 18s. to 20s. per gallon. Allowing for all expenses, including 'liberal consumption during manufacture', he estimates a profit of £8 to £10 from an outlay of 23s. The abolition of the Malt Tax in 1880 increased the gaugers' job of detection. Previously, the manufacture of malt, which occupied in all its stages some fourteen to twenty days, was illegal except by licensed traders, and during the manufacture, the smuggler was liable to detection. Now, malt could be made openly, or simply bought from dealers, so the smuggler could be caught only during the five or six days of brewing and distilling, or during the transportation of it.

But despite difficulties, seizures there were, although the Revenue officers were not always strong enough in number to arrest the actual offenders. He describes the discovery of an elaborate and well-equipped bothy high in the hills of Achanalt deer forest. The gaugers from Dingwall who found it thought they were too far from their colleagues to attempt the capture of the two operators who they thought might be joined by others at any moment. While they found no whisky, they took the all-important still, the head, and the worm. The smugglers had been in occupation for a considerable time. They had cut and dried peats solely for the use of their bothy, they had a kiln with perforated iron plates for drying their malt and had set up rollers to crush it. There was a sleeping bothy with beds made of dried grass and blankets and they had supplies of tea, bread, butter and sugar, and there were herring drying in the smoke of the still fire.

At the turn of the century, the remote glens and winding sea lochs of the west coast were the chief haunts of the smugglers. The gaugers had difficulty in penetrating these areas without being seen at some point in their journey and a warning being sent to the distillers. MacDonald tells of seizures and attempted seizures around Loch Torridon, Loch Druing, Inverasdale, Melvaig and Diabaig. The Inverasdale smugglers were very troublesome but Alligin, on Loch Torridon, was the only place where the Gairloch Revenue staff was deforced. They were prevented by force from entering a bothy, and, 'knowing the desperate character of the men, the unfriendly feeling of the whole township, the probability of help for the smugglers being near, and the risk of personal injuries, the officers desisted and duly reported the incident'. Across the hills from Alligin is Diabaig, 'another troublesome place' with very persistent smugglers. They had a saying in Diabaig – *is fada Diabaig bho lagh* – Diabaig is far from the law.

The situation as regards illicit distilling in the Highlands is quiet at the present time but who knows what might be aroused by further pressure of the 'fiscal hand'?

Notes to chapter

[1] Error for 'quaich', a drinking bowl.
[2] *Smuggling in the Highlands*, Ian MacDonald, Inverness, 1914.
[3] *Op. cit.*, p. 104.

5

Moonlight into Daylight

Let us now find the beginnings of the industry as we know it today. We have emphasized sufficiently the stupidity of the laws which drove whisky underground and made smuggling a necessity. Anyone who wanted good whisky had to drink smuggled whisky or make it himself. The traditional skills had to be kept alive by those who valued wholesome drink and had the qualities of courage and guile necessary to outwit the agents of the law. To seek for the birth of the modern industry we have to find the point at which the traditional craftsman, the skilled distiller, could practise his trade openly.

The 'breakthrough', if we can so call it, came through a Commission, headed by Lord Wallace, which sat from 1821 to 1823. The Act of Parliament which followed, while it did not by any means kill smuggling at one fell blow, at least made it possible to make good whisky openly. Some of those who had been driven to make good whisky in defiance of the law now came forward with the skills that they had preserved as outlaws and practised them with the blessing of the law.

The magic name in Highland whisky was Glenlivet. Famous people drank it, and in the early nineteenth century it was estimated that there were over two hundred illicit stills in the glen. Today, there are some twenty-eight distilleries which carry their own name hyphenated with that of Glenlivet. While this is a tribute to the just fame of the name, we must

88

remember that there is only one distillery in the parish of Glenlivet[1] and it is the only one which has the honour to carry the name 'The Glenlivet'. This has given rise to a rhymed saying:

> Glenlivet it has castles three
> Drumin, Blairfindy, and Deskie,
> And also one distillery
> More famous than the castles three.

It was only when the law was changed that a brave man, George Smith, decided to set up a legal distillery in the heart of this lawless district. The already famous Glenlivet whisky now acquired the accolade of legality. Sir Walter Scott paid tribute to the 'cunning chemists' of the glen, and in the year 1823, one year before the legal distillery of Glenlivet was built, he refers in his book *St. Ronan's Well* to a cordial prepared in the 'wilds of Glenlivet'. Sir Bingo treats the Captain and the Doctor to a cordial from the glen. They agree that it is the only drink fit for a gentleman in the morning and in the evening, and also that it is superior to all the wines of France for flavour, and besides, that it is more kindly to the system.

The neighbourhood of the valley of Glenlivet provided the four chief essentials of good whisky: good water, good barley, good peat, and Sir Walter's 'cunning chemists'. Fertile fields for the best high-starch barley were within its precincts, the stream of the Livet tumbled down twelve hundred feet from the Cairngorms, and from a northern newspaper of the early years of the nineteenth century, we learn that in this area 'everybody makes whisky and everyone drinks it'. From an Inverness newspaper in the year 1824, the year in which the Glenlivet distillery began its legal work, we learn that:

For a long time back, it was notorious that a large quantity of spirits were manufactured in Glenlivet – now the only district of the Highlands where this illicit and demoralising system is carried on to any great extent – and that the joint fruits of the smugglers' labour were carried to different parts of the low country by bands of people by far too numerous and powerful for any attempt at seizure by a single officer.

Among these smugglers had been George Smith. He must have been among 'the congregations of daring spirits', as a contemporary account describes them, 'in bands of ten to twenty men, with as many horses, with two ankers of whisky on the back of each horse, wending their way, singing in joyous chorus, along the banks of the Avon', taking the produce of the hills to the waiting Lowland markets. A son of a farmer, he was born in 1792 and trained as a builder and architect. He was also a scholar of Latin and had been brought up in the atmosphere of violence of the great smuggling age. About the year 1817, after the death of his father, he took over the family farm at Upper Drumin where he combined the traditional occupations of farming and smuggling.

George Smith was more far-sighted than his fellow smugglers. He saw that the new legislation of 1823, which sanctioned legal distilling, also made the production of good legal whisky possible. The Government itself had realized that it could not enforce an unpopular law in the Highlands without a greater cost than the revenue on distilling, or even fines on illegal distillers, could produce. The possibility of producing good whisky with a licence first occurred to George Smith. It is better to tell the story in his own words.

About this time, the Government giving its mind to internal reforms, began to awaken to the fact that it might be possible to realize a considerable revenue from the whisky duty north of the Grampians. No doubt they were helped to this conviction by the grumbling of the south country distillers whose profits were destroyed by the number of kegs which used to come streaming down the mountain passes. The Highlanders had become demoralized through long impunity and the authorities thought it would be safer to use policy rather than force. The question was frequently debated in both Houses of Parliament and strong representations made to north country proprietors to use their influence in the cause of law and order. Pressure of this sort was brought to bear on Alexander, Duke of Gordon, who was at length stirred up to make a reply. The Highlanders, he said, were born distillers: whisky was their beverage from time immemorial, and they would have it and sell it when tempted by so large a duty. But, said Duke Alexander, if the legislature would pass an Act affording an opportunity for the manufacture of whisky as good as the smuggled product at a reasonable duty easily payable, he and his brother proprietors of the Highlands would use their best endeavours to put down smuggling and encourage legal distilling. As the outcome of this pledge a bill was passed in 1823 to include Scotland, sanctioning legal distillation of whisky at a duty of 2s. 3d. per wine gallon of proof spirit with £10 annual licence for any still above forty gallons; none under that size being allowed.

This would seem a heavy burden to smuggling, and for a year or two before, the farce of an attempt had been made to inflict a penalty of £20 where any quantity of whisky was found manufactured or in process of manufacture. But there was no means of enforcing such a penalty for the smugglers laughed at attempts at seizure: when the new Act was heard of in Glenlivet and in the Highlands of Aberdeenshire, they ridiculed the idea that anyone should be found daring enough to start legal distilling in their midst. The proprietors were very anxious to fulfil their pledge to the Government and did everything they could to encourage the commencement of legal distilling; but the desperate character of the smugglers and the violence of their threats deterred anyone for some time. At length, in

1824, I, George Smith, who was then a robust young fellow and not given to be easily 'fleggit', determined to chance it. I was already a tenant of the Duke and received every encouragement from his Grace and his factor Mr. Skinner. The outlook was an ugly one, though. I was warned by my civil neighbours that they meant to burn the new distillery to the ground and me in the heart of it. The laird of Aberlour had presented me with a pair of hair trigger pistols worth ten guineas, and they were never out of my belt for years. I got together two or three stout fellows for servants, armed them with pistols, and let it be known everywhere that I would fight for my place to the last shot. I had a good character as a man of my word and, through watching by turns every night for years, we contrived to save the distillery from the fate so freely predicted for it. But I often, both at kirk and market, had rough times of it among the glen people; and if it had not been for the laird of Aberlour's pistols, I don't think I should be telling you this story now. In 1825 and 1826 three more legal distilleries were commenced in the glen, but the smugglers soon succeeded in frightening away their occupants, none of whom ventured to hang on a single year in the face of threats uttered so freely against them. Threats were not the only weapons used. In 1825 a distillery which had just been started near the Banks o' Dee at the head of Aberdeenshire was burnt to the ground with all its outbuildings and appliances and the distiller had a very narrow escape from being roasted in his own kiln. The country was in a very lawless state at this time. The riding officers of the Revenue were the mere sport of smugglers, and nothing was more common than for them to be shown a still at work and then coolly defied to make a seizure.

Smith's Glenlivet distillery survived, and survived as 'The Glenlivet'. It is difficult to say precisely what special quality it had. We know that it was famous in the 'heroic age' of whisky when it had virtually had to go underground. It carried its great name into the age when it was possible once again to make good whisky legally. It would seem, in this case at least, that honesty was the best policy. But the great name got its foundation in the smuggling era, and it is perhaps ironic that the man who fought for its establishment in the legal sense should have had to take legal action to protect the name of the glen which gave it birth. As we have said there are a number of hyphenated Glenlivets today. This does not mean, however, that these are vitally different from the Glenlivet itself. They are malt whiskies, produced with traditional care and respect, and all well worth drinking at their proper age.

Notes to chapter

[1] This no longer applies. Invergordon Distillers' Tamnavoulin-Glenlivet began production recently in this area.

6
Proof

Since the strength of Scotch whisky is a feature which interests many people, it is desirable to look at the concept of proof before looking at manufacture. Certainly it is something which, for many generations, has occupied the thoughts of those whose destiny it has been to wield the 'fiscal hand'. We have said already that the evolution of the whisky industry is milestoned through the years by the revenue legislation imposed upon it. But in order that legislation should continue comfortably, and that impositions should not multiply, the authorities had to arrive at a non-arbitrary and thoroughly practicable method of measuring the strength of whisky.

It seems that the first method of determining what came to be called 'proof' was by the inflammability of the spirit in question. A somewhat wasteful and crude process, though a roughly accurate one, was to take a measured quantity of the spirit and burn all the alcohol off it. Regarding the remaining liquid as water, and comparing it to the original quantity, one could then arrive at an estimate of the spirit's original strength.

Cruder, perhaps, was the method of soaking a cloth in the spirit and judging its strength by the readiness of the cloth to burn. There was yet another method by which one attempted to ignite gunpowder soaked in spirit. If this was difficult to do, the spirit was under-proof; if it burned with a steadfast flame, it was proof, and if it exploded, one decided that it was over-proof. Another device was the 'proof phial'. The spirit was poured briskly into a glass, shaken, and the accumulation of bubbles or 'beads' noted. These bubbles gather on the surface of a malt or grain whisky when the spirit is fairly strong. This was the first indication that the spirit was of a respectable strength. There followed an attempt to define that strength in more detail. This was done by noting the time that the bubbles took to disappear.

As these methods depended largely on a visual, and therefore a personal assessment of the steadiness of a flame or the strength of a 'bead', we can easily appreciate that they would not satisfy the growing appetite of the wolves of the Excise. The question of precise proof was open to argument between the distiller and the gauger. It was impossible, of course, to measure the strength of every drop that flowed from the still to the public drinker, and Exciseman and distiller had to agree or disagree over a sample. When spirit production and fiscal revenues swelled in the eighteenth century, a slight error or disagreement in estimating the strength of a spirit could mean the loss of a good lot of money to the distiller or to the Government. This was particularly true when small samples from large distillations were tested.

The authorities turned eagerly to the prospect of a scientific measuring instrument based on specific gravity. It seems that as early as the fifteenth century a certain gravity test was used by distillers. If oil of a given weight was added to a spirit, and it sank, the spirit was strong. If it floated, the spirit was weak. This method, however, had no precision and must be classed with the explosive, burning and 'bead' methods. It merely showed whether a spirit was strong or weak, and it could not measure degrees of strength or weakness.

The first man who invented a scientific instrument for measuring the strength of spirits with reasonable accuracy was a Londoner, John Clarke. He invented his 'Hydrometer and Brandy Prover' about 1725. He probably worked towards its improvement before he published his book under that title twenty-one years later in 1746. In this now very rare book, Clarke says that he was asked by some senior officials in the distilling business to 'contrive an instrument to ascertain the true strength of proof of brandy, rum, malt or molasses spirits, without tasting the same, or trusting to the uncertainty of the proof vial, the only method then made use of by the whole trade to discover whether any of the above mentioned liquors were proof or otherwise'.

He describes how at length he made such an instrument in copper and brass, which 'I brought to such perfection as not only to show the true proof of all the afore-mentioned liquors, but likewise, with great exactness to show the different degrees of strength, either under- or over-proof, from the strongest to the smallest that can be produced.'

This was obviously what was wanted. But although Clarke's hydrometer had been demonstrated before the Royal Society in 1730, the Government was remarkably slow to accept it. It was not until 1787 that it was legalized by Act of Parliament and then only until the fifth day of April 1788. By successive Acts it was legalized until 1801, when, for the time being, it was made permanent.

Despite this apparent permanence given to Clarke's hydrometer in 1801, there had been a clause in the 1787 Act which said that experiments should be conducted with all accurate hydrometers known, so that a suitable instrument be selected for estimating spirit values for revenue purposes. Indeed, while the acceptance of Clarke's hydrometer was going through its come-and-go stages in Parliament, there were movements to establish 'the best means of ascertaining the just proportion of duty to be paid by any kind of spirituous liquor that should come before the Officers of the Customs and Excise'. Perhaps the Government was suspicious that it was still being deprived of revenue. In 1790, at its request, it had a non-committal report from Sir Charles Blagden, President of the Royal Society, which said in substance that 'it is well known that no method admits of real accuracy but specific gravity'.

This led to a search for a method which would determine with the greatest possible accuracy the specific gravities of alcohol and water mixtures. 'An ingenious Swiss gentleman, Dr. Dolfuss' was given this task, but after he left the country George Gilpin, who had assisted him, carried on the work. The subsequent report of Gilpin and Blagden, published in 1794, laid the basis of any future assessment of this problem. In great detail they related the specific gravity of mixtures of water and alcohol for each degree of temperature from thirty degrees to eighty degrees Fahrenheit. Furthermore they related varying temperature to varying volume.

The result of this work, which was more detailed and advanced than Clarke's, was the establishment of a Committee of Enquiry in 1802. This committee had an assorted membership. Among others, there were Lord George Seymour, the Dean of Carlisle, John Grant, Surveyor of Excise in Leith, Mr. Smith a Member of Parliament, and Messrs. Berwell, Delafield, Parker, Phipps, Spiller and Jackson. Their brief was simple, to get something better than Clarke's hydrometer, and in August of the same year they advertised in the public press for offers of instruments for examination.

Among those who replied to this advertisement was one Bartholomew Sikes, an Exciseman who was already a recognized authority on this subject. In his application to the committee to have the instrument of his own development considered, and drawing on 'near half a century' of experience in the Excise, he said 'as if there be any part of knowledge in which I am more versed and fully grounded than any other, it is upon the subject of Hydrometers for ascertaining the strength of spirits, and for reducing or raising them from one degree of strength to any other required strength by means of water or other spirits of different strength'.

The committee had to arrive at a choice by an assessment,

not only of an instrument's accuracy, but also of its practicability. They selected eight instruments for test, and asked the makers of each to demonstrate their accuracy 'with as much dispatch as they could'. Consequently they were able to recommend to the Board of Excise that 'The Examiners of Hydrometers, in addition to the sketch which they have already presented respecting the accuracy of the instruments before them, are now enabled to make a further statement concerning the practical convenience of them.' They recommended the system of Bartholomew Sikes. The year was 1803, and in that year Sikes died. His widow was given a special grant of £2,000 in recognition of her husband's labours.

What is the situation today? I would like to quote from the booklet published by the Scotch Whisky Association, *Scotch Whisky, Questions and Answers* (Edinburgh, 1967). Of the testing of the strength of whisky and the methods used, it mentions the adoption of Clarke's hydrometer but goes on to say that a more accurate version by Bartholomew Sikes was universally adopted under the Hydrometer Act in 1818, and is in standard use today.

But what of the actual composition of the whisky that is called 'proof'? (And by the way, the word proof does not seem to be derived from the explosive sound 'poof' of the igniting gunpowder.) Proof spirit in the United Kingdom means that at a temperature of 51 degrees Fahrenheit, the spirit weighs exactly twelve-thirteenths of a volume of distilled water equal to the volume of the spirit. It is, in fact, a mixture of 57·1 per cent of alcohol and 42·9 per cent of water. That mixture is what we call proof in Britain. Varying strengths of proof are divided into degrees, and the normal strength at which whisky is sold to the public in this country is 30 degrees under-proof, proof being 100 degrees. I must emphasize, however, that this is the standard accepted in the United Kingdom. Many other countries prefer to state a percentage of alcohol, which is a very different matter. Even in countries where the concept of proof is used, as in the United States, the actual strength of proof can be different. Taking the latter-named country, for instance, 100 degrees proof spirit as defined there, is equivalent to 87·7 British proof, and the bottle of whisky out of which you take your tot, marked in this country 70 degrees proof would, in America, be marked 80 degrees.

The normal methods of assessing alcohol strengths generally used on the Continent are: the Gay Lussac system – France and Belgium; the Tralles system – Austria, Italy and Russia; and the Windisch system – Germany. Both the Gay Lussac and the Tralles systems estimate alcoholic strength by volume per cent, the former at a temperature of 59 degrees Fahrenheit and the latter at 60 degrees. They are thus very close to one another. For instance, 70 British Sikes proof is equivalent to 39·9 per cent Gay Lussac and 41·1 per cent Tralles. The German Windisch system estimates alcohol by weight per cent and the equivalent of 70 British proof is Windisch 33·4 per cent.

Because of its simplicity in comparison to the Sikes system, recommendations have been made to have Gay Lussac adopted in Great Britain and in America. Yet there would not seem to be any great practical advantages in adopting any system alternative to proof in this country. Through trade diaries the trade itself is perfectly at home with the various conversion tables which give keys to the various systems, and the man in the pub would certainly raise his eyebrows at finding 39·9 per cent on his bottle instead of the traditional 70° proof.

7

The Making of Whisky

There are not many secrets in the making of good Scotch whisky. It is true that a great deal of skill is required during the various phases of its manufacture, but there is no question of any sort of secret formula being used except, perhaps, in the sales promoter's talk. The imponderables of good distilling are only secret in the sense that we do not fully understand them. These can make a tantalizing difference between whiskies from neighbouring distilleries, and this difference of flavour and bouquet does not make one whisky good and the other bad. It is true that the countries to which whisky is not a traditional drink do not seem to be able to make it satisfactorily. Perhaps this is due to climatic differences or to the lack of the traditional skills which are necessary rather than to the lack of knowledge of the principles of malting, brewing, still measurements, temperatures etc. To establish whether or not it is possible to make, say, a good Highland malt whisky in a European country, one should export an integrated whisky-making team to see what they could do.

Certainly, it does not seem to be necessary for any distiller, Highland or Lowland, to cloud his activities in mystery, and to say this does not detract in any way from the subtlety of the ancient skills which go towards its manufacture. With the blender it is a different matter. When, after a good deal of painstaking sampling, he has hit on a good formula involving up to forty-five or so single whiskies, he is not likely to hand it on a plate to anyone.

While our whisky is called Scotch throughout the world, there is neither mystique nor nationalism in the distiller's choice of his basic product, barley. He is guided by scientific principles and barley grown in Scotland is not always the best for this purpose. The distiller is looking for a grain which has plenty of starch in it with a low nitrogen and protein content. It must have a high germination value as it has to germinate during the malting process. It must be well ripened, and dryness is important so that it can be stored without becoming mouldy. So Scottish barley is not always the best and today much of it comes from the Continent and from Australia.

The first thing that happens to barley in the distillery is screening for impurities. This is done by passing it through dressing machines which pass it by conveyor belts to storing lofts. It is then steeped in vessels containing spring or burn water and in some cases having coils containing air jets which agitate the water and separate the lighter, bad quality grains from the heavier. These steeping vessels normally deal with some twenty-five bushels of grain each and the grain stays in them for between 52 to 62 hours. A bushel is 55 lb. After steeping, the barley goes direct to the cement malting floors where it is at first stacked in heaps about three feet high. What follows depends a good deal on temperatures, and practice can vary between different distilleries. The barley can spend from 18 to 48 hours in heaps of this kind until small bud-like protrusions can be seen at the germ end. It is then thinned out by the maltmen and its germinating time is estimated from this point. To keep it at a suitable and even temperature, of about 60° F., the malt is constantly turned, in many cases manually, by men using 'shiels' – large wooden shovels specially designed for this purpose. Warm, humid weather is the maltman's worst enemy and this is one important reason why many distilleries with their own maltings go 'silent', or cease production, for some two months during the warmest part of the summer. At an appropriate time, usually between eight and twelve days, the change to malt is held to be complete. The developing rootlets wither and the grain becomes mealy. The object of the malting process is the production of the enzyme amylase, which begins the conversion of the starch of the barley into sugar. An enzyme is a chemical or unorganized ferment, as distinguished from the living ferment yeast, which comes into the process later. When the malted barley, or 'green malt' as it is called, is judged ready for the next phase, it is transferred to a kiln for drying.

The kiln, with its distinctive pagoda-type head, is the most prominent feature of the malt distillery and it is at this stage that the distinctive peaty flavour of a Highland whisky is introduced. The green malt is spread on perforated iron sheets through which the heat and smoke of peat is percolated. The peat is not used throughout the whole process of drying but generally only at the beginning when it is more readily absorbed by the moist husk of the grain. Afterwards, when the temperature is raised for the final drying off, coke, sometimes with an admixture of peat, is used. This final heating, reaching a temperature of about 160 degrees Fahrenheit, lasts about fifty-six hours. This drying process, besides imparting a peaty flavour to the whisky which never leaves it throughout distillation, also kills the germ of the growing grain while only modifying the enzymes present in it. The drying must be carefully controlled to maintain the activity of the enzymes and their potentiality to convert the starch of the malted grain later into sugar, or *maltose*. The brewer of beer, for instance, heats his malt to a higher temperature because he does not want his enzymes fully active. He is aiming at the production, not of maltose, but at a form of *dextrin*. You may know dextrin as the soluble sticky substance used on the back of adhesive stamps.

After the kiln stage, the malt is left for a period of some

six weeks, during which time it is screened from impurities and separated from its dried-up rootlets. These become a cattle food sold under the name of *malt culms*. Before the sugar and the other soluble substances in the malt can be extracted it has to be ground into a rough meal.

The ground malt, or *grist*, is now ready for the *mashing* process. It is placed in large circular mash tuns. These vessels vary very much in size, from the single 1,000-gallon one at Edradour, probably the smallest distillery in Scotland, to several of 5,000 gallons or over. Here, the grist is extracted four times with hot water, each filling of water having its own set temperature. The first filling can be as low as 140° F., although 155° F. might be considered nearer the norm. The second water is some twelve degrees higher and the third and fourth higher still in proportion. Some distilleries use only three fillings and the following temperatures are used at William Grant's Lowland Malt Distillery at Ladyburn in Ayrshire – 144° F., 166° F., and 175° F. It is the temperature of the first extraction which is most important. Only the first two extractions pass on to the fermentation stage. The third and the fourth, known collectively as *sparge*, are held back to form the first and second extractions of the next batch of grist. The purpose of the mashing operation is to reactivate the chemical ferments or enzymes which were inhibited during the drying process and allow them to continue their work of extracting the malt sugar and other soluble substances.

The first two extractions from the mash tun are collectively called *wort* and they contain all the sugars of the malt and some secondary constituents. The distiller has no further use for the barley and it is now sold as cattle food under the name of *draff*. This is sometimes dried and sold as distillery grains, similar to the brewers' grains available from breweries. The length of a mashing operation can take from eight to ten hours.

The saccharine liquid called wort is cooled to a temperature of 70 to 80° F. by passing it through a heat exchanger. This is a temperature at which the yeast can safely operate. It is pumped immediately into the fermenting vats, or *washbacks*. These can vary from 1,000-gallon capacity as at Edradour to a capacity of well over 10,000 gallons. For instance, the modern Deanston distillery has eight fermenting vats, each of which can take a 13,000-gallon fermentation. These are fourteen feet in diameter and seventeen and a half feet in depth. In the older distilleries the washbacks are usually made of larch or Oregon pine, but in new or renovated distilleries one tends to find them made of Corten steel, sometimes, as at Deanston, with timber covers. In these vessels yeast of a suitable strain is added to the wort after care has been taken to prevent it undergoing secondary fermentation from the wild yeasts which are found in most distilleries. The vats are never filled up to the top since some space must be left for the agitation caused by the yeast and the emission of carbon dioxide. Mechanical arms or switches revolve constantly to keep the heaving wort from overflowing. It is at this stage that the most familiar odour of a distillery is produced. The great quantity of carbon dioxide coming from the fermenting vats is usually treated as a waste product, but at some distilleries such as Littlemill and Loch Lomond, use is made of it.

The Excise officer comes into the operation at the beginning of this process. With the distiller he calculates the approximate quantity of spirit that the wort should yield, from the specific gravity of the liquid at the beginning of fermentation and at the end. The purpose of fermentation by yeast is, of course, the conversion of the sugar into alcohol and carbon dioxide. The density of the liquid falls as this conversion takes place, and the yield of proof spirit from the fermenting wort can be estimated by the rate of fall of its density. The yield of alcohol is one proof gallon from each 100 gallons of wort for every five degrees of difference between the highest and the lowest readings. Let us take as an easy example two likely readings in round figures, a specific gravity of 1·045 at the beginning of fermentation, falling to 0·995 at the end. The difference being 50 degrees, we should expect the final distillation to yield ten gallons of proof spirit for every hundred gallons of wort. There is a rise of some twenty degrees in temperature during the forty hours or so required for fermentation. The final liquid containing crude alcohol and other substances is now called *wash* and is the liquid which is to enter the actual stills.

The saccharine solution produced by the chemical ferment of the enzymes in the malt has now been subject to the living ferment of the yeast and turned into a weak alcoholic liquid, the food that the pot stills are waiting for. In the description that follows of the distillation stage in a pot still, general terms are used and these will be amplified later by reference to particular distilleries.

The most prominent objects inside a malt distillery are the two pear-shaped pot stills, one a *wash* still and the other a *low-wines* still. The wash still is the bigger of the two. It has to deal with the crude mixture of alcohol and other substances which comes direct from the fermentation stage. This contains a great many unwanted impurities and the object of the first distillation is to separate as pure a spirit as possible from this weak ale. The wash still may have a capacity of 5,000 gallons, as at Loch Lomond, although 3,500 gallons will be nearer the norm. At the other extreme is the wash still at the small distillery already mentioned, Edradour, which has an overall capacity of 750 gallons. But even this small figure is a false one. The manager, Mr. Warren, explained to me that with the recent addition of internal heating coils, the actual capacity of the still was much less. In the older type of still, external heating by coal is used, although new stills and some of the renovated ones use internal steam coils.

On our first page we referred to the process of distillation as that of 'separating the different elements in a liquid by volatilization and condensation', i.e. vaporizing a liquid and subsequently recovering part of it by condensation. This is what happens in the pot still. The wash, which in the barest definition is a mixture containing alcohol, is heated to a point above the boiling point of alcohol and below that of water. This, however, is an over-simplified statement. The boiling point of alcohol is 78° C. and that of water 100° C., and much depends on the proportion of water to alcohol in the original mixture. For example, if the wash contains 50 per cent of each, it will vaporize at 83·1° C., if 60 per cent water and 40 per cent alcohol it will vaporize at 84·1° C. As the whisky wash is a weak wash which is not strengthened by the addition of any extraneous materials, the temperature in the still will be much nearer the boiling point of water.

Inside the wash still is a *rummager*, consisting of four rotating arms controlling a copper chain mesh which is dragged around the bottom of the still. This prevents insoluble bodies in the wash from burning on the still bottom. Distillation continues in the wash still until all the alcohol has been driven off and collected in one distillate known as *low wines*. The liquor remaining in the still is called *pot ale*, or *burnt ale*, and is usually run to waste.

Before the distillate is achieved, the boiling wash has had to be condensed and this is done by means of the *worm*, a coiled copper pipe of decreasing diameter enclosed in a tub or container through which cold water circulates. As the contents of the still vaporize, a good deal of froth may be produced and this is controlled by inserting a special kind of soap at the rate of eight ounces per five thousand gallons. On their way from the wash still the low wines pass through the *spirit safe*, a locked brass case with glass windows, supervised by the Excise and containing thermometers and hydrometers which indicate specific gravity and make it obvious when all alcohol has been removed from the still. The proportion of the weak spirit called *low wines* coming over is usually just under one-quarter of the original volume of the contents. For a 5,000-gallon still this stage can take eight hours.

On leaving the still and passing through the condensing worm the distillate enters a receiving tank where it is mixed with the *foreshots* and *feints*, i.e. the rejected portions of the second distillation. It then passes to a tank called the low-wines charger, which as its name implies, charges the second still, the low-wines still. This still, which is sometimes called a spirit still, is smaller than the wash still because it does not have to deal with such a large charge. The following are some actual figures of the difference in capacity between these two stills at the time of writing and they give an indication of the general relationship between them. Loch Lomond, 5,000–2,500 gallons; Glenmorangie, 3,500–2,500; Deanston, same capacities but two of each are used; Edradour, 740–420; Isle of Jura, 7,680–3,750.

Besides being smaller, the spirit still has no need of a rummager because it is dealing with a liquid with few solid bodies. The produce of this still is fractionated into three sections. The first runnings to come over, the foreshots, are diverted by the stillman to the low-wines receiving tank to undergo the second distillation again together with the next charge of low wines. It is the responsibility of the stillman, watching the brass box and manipulating the flows, to decide when the runnings become potable. Speaking generally, it is the centre portion that is selected and diverted to the spirit receiving tank. This comes over at 25 to 26 over-proof and is collected while it is decreasing in strength down to 5 over-proof. The stillman rejects the final runnings called feints and these also find their way back to await further distillation. He controls the distillation, however, right down to water gravity to show that no further alcohol is left. What is left in the still now is mostly water, although there may be some copper in solution from the pot itself. This is called *spent lees* and, like the pot ale, is run to waste. The time taken in this second distillation depends a lot on still capacity and the cooling capacity of the water in the condenser. If a distillation should take nine hours to complete, the production of the potable spirit would take five hours of this period. The temperature at which the low wines vaporize is much lower than that of the wash. The latter must be heated to several degrees over 200 degrees Fahrenheit whereas low wines can begin to vaporize as low as 165 degrees.

The pot still we have been discussing has not changed its design for centuries and it seems to be directly descended from the alembics of the alchemists. The most important part of the still is the head or top, and the angle of the *lyne arm*, a wide-diameter pipe connecting the head to the condensing unit, can affect the distillate greatly. And we must remember that the distillers of Scotch whisky are not aiming at the production of what is called 'pure' alcohol. Such alcohol does not contain the elements that the palate finds desirable.

When the stills have finished with it, the bright, clear new whisky is barrelled in wood. Sherry-treated wood is the most prized and there is no doubt that a first filling after sherry makes the aged whisky most palatable. These barrels are scarce now and charred American barrels are used. According to American law, Bourbon barrels can be used once only and accordingly there is a surplus of them. Some distillers with business affiliations with American distillers are particularly fortunate in this respect.

Before going to the warehouses for maturing, some spring water is added to the new whisky. The potable centre section of the second distillation has been selected all the way from its beginning at 25 over-proof down to the strength at which the flow is directed to the low-wines receiver as feints, i.e. about 5 over-proof and the section as a whole will probably average about 16 over-proof. The addition of the spring water is calculated to bring it down to between 11 and 12 over-proof, and this is the strength at which it enters its period of maturation although when speaking in the trade of its quantity and strength, it is always referred to in proof gallons. It is double-locked in bonded store with the Exciseman holding one set of keys and there it will remain for a number of years until it is released to be sold under its own name as a single malt whisky, or, much more likely, to be blended into one of the household names of Scotch whisky. By law, the whisky must be matured for a minimum period of three years, but there is no malt whisky that I know that could remotely approach its best during the short period of three years, no matter how well it was kept.

There is no fixed 'best' age for malt whisky. A number of factors must be taken into consideration. A great deal depends on the size and nature of the cask, and the humidity of the store in which the whisky is lying. The same spirit kept in a sherry cask and in a plain cask will not be the same after a few years, and this can be said also of whisky in different sizes of casks and in warehouses of differing humidity. These variable factors – plain and sherry casks, large and small casks, and wet and dry warehouses – are all taken into account in Ireland when a blend of Irish whiskey is being prepared for the market.

Speaking generally, it can be said that some of the lighter-character malts can reach their best at seven to eight years, and in some cases can be potable at five. Others take ten to twelve years, and while one must approach a Macallan-Glenlivet or The Glenlivet after spending fifteen years in the atmosphere of the Central Highlands with great reverence, I personally find that Dalmore after twelve years in sherry wood is quite superb. But one cannot be so bold as to declare which whisky is the best, or range them in a fixed order of quality.

It is the practice, however, to divide them into three main groups – Highland, Lowland, and West Highland. The first group are those which are made north of an imaginary line drawn from Greenock to Dundee and they may be divided into Glenlivets and Highland. The fame of The Glenlivet caused many others to incorporate the name in their own, sometimes without a hyphen. In 1860 the proprietor of Smith's took legal action to protect the name, and won a decision that no one except The Glenlivet distillery could use the name without a hyphen.

Lowland malt is made south of the line mentioned above. There is no difference in the method of manufacture from that practised in the Highlands. Indeed some use peat to lend flavour to their product, while some Highland distillers are abandoning the use of peat in the interests of 'lightness' in their whisky. Lowland malt is very amenable to blending and is much in demand for that purpose. West Highland malt is made mostly in the island of Islay and with them are grouped the two distilleries in Campbeltown in Kintyre, although some people in the trade make a generic distinction between them. They are heavily peated, strongly flavoured, and tend to dominate a blend unless used very carefully. The distinction between Highland and West Highland is not a straightforward geographical one. The Talisker of the Isle of Skye, for instance, is classed as a Highland, and the whisky from the recently built distillery on the Isle of Jura will undoubtedly reach its maturity with more kinship to the Highland group than to the West Highland.

The above description of malt distilling in pot stills corresponds to general practice in Scotland. There are, however, one or two stills that use a *triple* distillation in their operations and not a double one as described above. One of these is the Lowland malt still of Auchentoshan in Dunbartonshire.[1] Its history is interesting (see Ross Wilson in *Wine and Spirit Trade Record*, January 1968) in that it gave prime importance to the brewing stage of the operation, to providing the best wash for the distilling stage. Auchentoshan's approach to mashing is interesting and the familiar three to four extractions of the malt with hot water is not carried out here. Instead, the mash tun receives one charge of hot water which is stirred or mashed for twenty minutes and then left to stand or infuse for one hour. Only this single charge goes forward from the mash tuns to the washbacks for ultimate distillation. Finally a sparging process is carried out which will act as the liquor for the next mashing.

We now come to the unusual process of distillation at Auchentoshan, where three pot stills, each with their own particular function, are used instead of the more normal two. It has a wash still, a low-wines still and a spirit still. The wash still is charged with some two thousand gallons of wash. Its purpose is to produce low wines which have passed through a kind of rectifying apparatus, thus eliminating some undesirable higher alcohols. The low-wine still is then charged with some 1,800 gallons of the low wines thus produced. Normally, the 'middle run' of such a distillation would be taken as the final spirit. But Auchentoshan at this stage is content with separating the strongest and purest low wines and feints from the cruder elements. The distillate of the low wines still varies from 5 over-proof at its weakest to 50 over-proof at its strongest. Anything under 5 over-proof is sent back to the low-wines receiver to be re-distilled and anything over that strength goes forward to the spirit still. Some 1,000 gallons of these relatively pure low wines pass into the spirit still, and despite this comparatively small amount, it takes as long as nine hours to distil it. The selected fraction of the final spirit is taken at an average of 45 over-proof.

There is no great variation in price between the whiskies which we have been discussing. These are the prices quoted for a selection of them in November 1969; they are for whiskies of the current season, all prices per proof gallon. Eight Highland malts can be had for 13s. per gallon. This is the lowest price quoted. Most of the Highland, Lowland, and West Highland malts come in at between 14s. and 16s. per gallon. Five, Tormore, Talisker, Ardmore, Macallan-Glenlivet, and Laphroaig (Islay), are quoted at 16s.; Glen Grant and The Glenlivet at 16s. 3d., and, if you want to pay the top price of 16s. 9d., you will have to ask for the rare potion of Edradour.[2] Keep in mind, however, that these are prices in bond, and if you want to take them out of bond, you will have to pay the Chancellor of the Exchequer £17 13s. 9d. per proof gallon.

You may choose from eight Lowland malt distilleries and ninety-seven Highland.

So far we have spoken about malt, or pot still whisky only. Grain, or patent still whisky is just as important as malt whisky to the modern Scotch whisky industry, though not in its own right as a single spirit. It costs about half of the former for blending purposes, the opening prices at the moment ranging from 6s. 9d. to 8s. per proof gallon. Grain whisky is sometimes called *silent spirit*, or simply *fillings*.

The patent still is a continuously working unit, as distinct from the pot still, which, by virtue of its two separate distillations, is interrupted. The first still of this kind appears to have been invented by the well-known Scots distiller Robert Stein. He had one in operation at the distillery of Kirkliston before 1831. It was not as successful, however, as the one patented in July 1832 by Aeneas Coffey, Inspector General of the Excise in Ireland. This apparatus came into such widespread use in Scotland that the patent still is now quite commonly referred to as the 'Coffey' still. There are different ones of Continental design, Barbet and Ilye being perhaps the best known. The still itself consists of two tall copper columns, each between forty and fifty feet high, one called the *analyser*, and the other the *rectifier*. The columns are rectangular in shape and are divided horizontally into chambers with perforated copper bottoms, each fitted with a drip pipe into the chamber below. This apparatus can distil rapidly and continuously a spirit of over 90 per cent alcoholic content.

The patent still does not use the same mash as the pot still. It only uses some 20 per cent malted barley, the rest being made up of unmalted cereals, usually maize, although barley, wheat, rye or oats can also be used. The pre-distilling phase is roughly similar to that of the pot still method. The malted barley is milled into grist while the unmalted grain is cooked in convertors for three and a half hours under a pressure of 38–40 pounds per square inch. This is done in order to burst its starch cells so that the enzymes of the malt can have proper access to all particles of the grain. While it is sometimes thought that the malted barley is introduced into the patent still process in order to lend some character to the final product, its real purpose is to bring about chemical changes in the maize necessary for fermentation. Maize has a higher alcohol yield than barley but needs the stimulus of the malt to aid in its conversion. Mashing is carried out in a similar way to that in the malt distilleries though on a much larger scale. The fermentation stage is also similar, but the difference in scale can be appreciated if we realize that a grain distillery can have sixteen fermenting vats capable of fermenting nearly a million gallons per week.

Before the wash goes to the distilling apparatus it is preheated by passing it through a closed pipe encased in the steam-laden rectifier column. In some cases it may be pre-heated by passing it through a dephlegmator. It then goes to the top of the analyser column, which, like the rectifier column, has been filled with steam under pressure. As the wash enters the top of the analyser column, it meets this rising pressurized steam which prevents it passing the perforated plate which forms the base of the chamber. It can only pass when its level reaches that of the drip pipe, about an inch above the base plate. This process is repeated in each chamber, and, as the boiling point of steam is, of course, above the vaporizing temperature of alcohol, by the time the wash reaches the bottom of the analyser, it has been robbed of its volatile elements by the ascending steam and is practically free from alcohol. This alcoholic steam which remains in the analyser contains undesirable higher alcohols as well as the desirable potable ethyl alcohol. To remove these is the purpose of the rectifier. The steam passes from the base of the analyser to the base of the rectifier and begins to ascend that column chamber by chamber. These secondary alcohols have a different condensation point from that of ethyl, and as the vapour ascends through the varying cooling temperatures of the different chambers the latter is isolated at a certain point in the column, which corresponds in temperature to the condensation temperature of strong ethyl alcohol. At this point, a copper sheet pierced by a wide pipe replaces the perforated sheets of the other chambers. This traps the condensing ethyl alcohol and conducts it to the cooling worm.

Grain whisky is matured in a similar way and at the same alcoholic strength as malt whisky, despite its much greater strength on leaving the worm. Since the rectifying element has removed many of the secondary constituents found in the malt spirit, it does not require the same ageing. This is also why grain spirit is sometimes called *silent spirit*. This term is rather misleading as there is quite a pronounced difference between grain whiskies from different distilleries, both in their raw and matured states. Some make more appeal to blenders than others do and this facet of them is reflected in different prices in the trade.

In our description of the processes above, we have not mentioned the part played by chemists. Chemists have been abroad in the whisky distilleries for generations but never in the same numbers as at the present time. Perhaps their chief function in the production process is the development of yeast strains. They also measure alcoholic strength with laboratory precision, and chemical analysts are required for the preparation of export certificates. Furthermore they are interested in the secondary constituents of whisky. Some of these may be harmful while others give it that bouquet which absolute alcohol could never possess. They include volatile acids which form esters (or 'ethers' as they are sometimes called in the trade) when they condense with alcohol, aldehydes, which are formed by the oxidation of alcohol, and our familiar fusel oil. The latter is, of course, absent from grain whisky, as is the aldehyde furfurol when it is new, although it appears slightly after maturation. This aldehyde is present in malt whisky at all stages of maturation. Other items to be analysed are amounts of tannin, artificial colouring, copper from the pot, and the amount of solid matter in general in the finished product. Solid matter rarely amounts to more than two parts per thousand at proof. The total amount of solid matter in malt whisky is reckoned to be over 500 parts per 100,000 of alcohol, while in grain whisky, it is estimated as being as low as 100. Many reasons are given for this disparity. In the case of the higher alcohols it is quite explicable, as these are drawn off in the patent still. Some variation must also arise from the difference in the mashes that the washes are prepared from. The 'cooking' of the wash which takes place in the pot still is also thought by some to contribute to the proportion of secondary elements in the final product.

One thing is quite certain. It is not yet possible to define the character of a given whisky in the quantitative terms of the chemist's analysis. A chemist without a 'nose', no matter how skilful, cannot give an opinion from his analysis as to the impact of that whisky on the palate.

Notes to chapter

[1] I have had the pleasure of sampling this excellent whisky at five years old, and at 5 over-proof. It should be bottled as a single malt.

[2] There is little variation in the opening prices for 1970. Edradour has now advanced to 17s. 6d. per gallon while five other Highland malts have advanced to 17s. Only one can now be had at 13s.

8

Whisky, Whiskey and Usquebaugh

The term 'whiskey' is now reserved exclusively for the Irish spirit, and it is over fifty years since the spelling 'whisky' came into fixed use in Scotland. During the first decade or so of this century, the former spelling was used indiscriminately for Irish and Scotch. Yet in 1878, when four Irish distilling companies published the book *Truths about Whisky*, the spelling 'whisky' was used throughout when referring to the Irish product. The fixed use of the other term is apparently intended to indicate that the Irish product is different from the Scotch. This is quite true. Though the processes of manufacture are similar in many ways, the final product is fundamentally different.

The raw materials are different to begin with. Some malted barley is used, but it is supplemented by unmalted barley, rye, wheat, and oats. It is thus surprising to find a respected connoisseur like the late Maurice Healy saying in his book *Stay me with Flagons*, that you can drink Irish whiskey in the knowledge that 'nothing but malted barley has gone into the mash from which it was distilled' (p. 227). The contrary is openly stated by Irish distillers. The barley which is normally used is that of the hybrid Spratt-Archer variety and grown in Ireland. When it comes into the distillery it contains from seventeen to twenty per cent moisture, and would be in danger of going mouldy in store unless kiln dried. The portion of it which is

116

intended for malting is dried down to twelve per cent moisture, and the portion of it which is selected for mashing in the unmalted state is dried down to six per cent. The former type of drying is known as 'sweating', as distinct from the 'high drying' of the portion which is reduced to six per cent, and it must be done slowly at a temperature not exceeding 110° F., so as not to injure the embryo in the grain. This sweating process hastens the end of the dormant period in it although it is allowed to rest for three weeks before malting.

The malting stage is similar to that in Scotland, and in this and in the kiln drying of the green malt, the Irish distiller is aiming at a malt with as high a diastatic power as possible. We must remember that it not only has to convert its own starch into sugar, but also act on the unmalted grain in a similar way. No peat is used in the Irish malt-drying kiln.

For the mashing stage, the various grains, except the oats which are merely crushed, are ground very finely, much more so than the malt is ground in Scotland. The grains then pass to the *kieve*, or mash tun, which with its false bottoms and revolving rakes, is similar in pattern to those in Scotland. Waters of successively higher temperatures are used to separate the maltose from the malt. The first extraction is interesting. The kieve receives its first charge of ground grain while water simultaneously enters through the bottom until the vessel is half-full. After over an hour, a second charge of water at a higher temperature is added and the kieve is filled to the brim. After settling for half an hour, the wort is drained off, at first from the top of the kieve and later through the perforated bottom. Here we see the function of the roughly crushed oats. They prevent the finely ground grains from clogging and inhibiting drainage. The further three extractions at higher temperatures are kept aside, as the last two are in Scotland, for use in the next mash, and the spent grains are sold to farmers as cattle food.

The cooled wort from the first mashing is mixed with yeast in the familiar way, but in much larger vessels. In an Irish distillery one can meet fermenting backs capable of holding over 33,000 gallons of wort. In fact there are eleven of these in John Jameson's of Dublin. The process takes about seventy-two hours, and when the gravity has fallen as low as possible, the wash is now ready for distillation. This further process is different from that in Scotland.

Visiting an Irish distillery for the first time, a Scotsman is immediately impressed by the largeness of the distilling pots. They are fundamentally the same in appearance, but in Ireland a wash still can hold over 25,000 gallons. In John Jameson's there are two of these, and two low-wines stills with a capacity of 15,000 gallons each. This is an important point of difference. MacIan, in his book *Highlanders at Home*, published in 1848, remarked on the belief that small still spirits were superior and commented on the factors which were supposed to establish this superiority. He accepted the supposition that the *braich*, or malt, was supposed to be of better quality 'since it is made in smaller quantities and is very carefully attended to'. Generally speaking, one must suppose that a small quantity can be more meticulously handled than a large quantity, and certainly the malt distillers of Scotland seem to prefer a multiplicity of small stills to a lesser number of larger ones. This is true even of distilleries with a considerable output. The modern distillery at Deanston, near Stirling, has two wash stills of 3,500 gallons each and two low-wines stills of 2,500 gallons. Yet it is capable of an output of 900,000 proof gallons in a forty-four-week year, without, as Mr. Geddes the manager picturesquely put it, 'pushing the pot'. These comments are not intended to indicate any difference of quality between the national beverages of the two nations, but simply to emphasize that Irish and Scotch are two quite different drinks.

A difference in treatment develops also at the distilling stage. This is more complicated than in Scotland and is virtually a triple distillation. It is not that the triple distillation was unknown in Scotland. On the contrary, it seems to have been quite common, and one of the earliest Scottish Gaelic words for whisky, if not the earliest, is not *uisge-beatha*, the water of life, but *treas tarruing* – thrice distilled or drawn.

The Irish pot still is heated both by steam coils and by fire underneath. Despite the more modern type of heating, the external fire is still considered an essential part of pot distilling. There is some dispute in Scotland whether this can affect the flavour of the product. The theory that the 'cooking' of the wash as it comes into contact with the hot casing of the pot has a beneficial effect on the distillate, still has its adherents, and they would approve of the Irish technique here. The external fire necessitates a mechanical device for scraping the convex upward bottom of the still to prevent solid particles in the wash charring. The vapour from the still enters the horizontal pipe called the lyne arm on its way to the worm. This is immersed in a tank of cold water and some preliminary condensation takes place. Presumably this liquid is unwanted, since it is returned to the still through a pipe known as a 'foul pipe'. While this feature is not traditional in Scotch production, Long John's Lowland malt plant at Kinclaith uses a water jacket on the lyne arm and some unwanted condensate is returned to the still. The vapour then proceeds to the worm, coils of copper piping decreasing in diameter from fourteen inches at the top to six inches at the bottom, and encased in the cylindrical tank known as the worm tub. The liquor emerging from the worm is, as in Scotland, called 'low wines', but is collected in two fractions, a strong one at an average strength of just under-proof, and a weaker one going down to an average of 75 under-proof. The total bulk of the low wines collected is about one-third of the original volume of the wash in the still. The spent wash finds some market among farmers, who use it in mixing hot foods for their cattle.

The low wines are distilled again, and here we find a similar technical vocabulary to that in Scotland, but with a somewhat different application. The distillation of the stronger sections of the low wines yields feints. This is again collected in two fractions, the stronger averaging about 30 over-proof and the weaker about 75 under-proof. Then the strong portion of the feints is distilled yet again, and the first portion called *first-shot*, the Scottish 'foreshot', is rejected because of its higher alcohols and other undesirable substances, and only the centre section of this triple-distilled spirit is finally selected for maturation. When it passes out of the worm for the last time the whiskey is about 50 over-proof as against a maximum of some 25 over-proof in Scotland. A further difference is that it is diluted for maturation purposes to 25 over-proof only as distinct from 11 to 12 over-proof. The Irish also use sherry casks when they can get them, and they mature their product in bonded warehouses for a minimum period of seven years.

Despite the similarity in apparatus and traditions, the two products are very different and it is difficult to see any precise reason for this divergence. To complicate this already complex question, there is the fact that the founder of the great Irish distilling house of John Jameson's of Dublin was John Jameson, ex-Sheriff Clerk of Alloa in the county of Clackmannan, Scotland – a Scotsman born and bred. He came to Dublin with his two sons in the late 1770s. Did he plant in Ireland distilling methods then prevalent in Scotland or did he follow an already existing technique? Who knows?

It only remains to be said that the Irish whiskey one sees in bottle in Ireland or out of it, is a single pot still whiskey and not a blend of pot and patent still spirits such as the best known Scotch brands are. Blending the products of the two types of still, though not by any means unknown in Ireland, just has not caught on. When the word 'blend' is used on an Irish label, it indicates a mixture of different matured types of the same whiskey. In discussing the maturing of Scotch malt whisky, we noted the different effects of varying cask sizes and types, and humid and non-humid warehouses. These variable factors which affect the produce of an individual distillery are very carefully noted when bottling Irish whiskey.

Traditionally, Irish distillers have not been as highly organized commercially as those of Scotland. In earlier times, England appears to have been a good market for Irish whiskey although the extent to which it was drunk without being further rectified or compounded is uncertain. The word 'usquebaugh', the English corruption of the Irish Gaelic for 'aqua vitae', signified in most cases a liquor re-distilled and compounded with spices and aromatic seeds. Many recipes for it exist in eighteenth- and nineteenth-century books. In D. H. Smith's *Compleat Body of Distilling* published in 1729, a number are given, including one which uses six gallons of proof malt spirit and five of proof molasses spirit. No source is given for the spirit, although it is interesting to see that in his instructions for preparing the usquebaugh, he refers to both as 'brandy'. This term brandy appears to have had a wide reference. In his book *Tour Through Great Britain*, Daniel Defoe makes a special reference to 'Glasgow Brandy': 'there is a large distillery for distilling spirits from the molasses drawn from the sugars and which they call Glasgow Brandy . . .'. However, in Smith's recipe, the spirits are re-distilled with mace, cloves, coriander seeds, raisins, dates, liquorice, and ten pounds of Lisbon sugar, the whole distillate to be run through four ounces of the best English saffron 'hung at the worm's end'. A. Cooper, whose book *The Complete Distiller* has been mentioned in the opening chapter, says 'Usquebaugh is a very celebrated cordial, the basis of which is saffron.' He gives recipes for Common Usquebaugh, Royal Usquebaugh, and French Usquebaugh. For the making of ten gallons of common usquebaugh he recommends two ounces each of nutmegs, cloves and cinnamon, four ounces each of the seeds of anise, caraway and coriander, a half a pound of sliced liquorice root. The seeds and spices are to be bruised and put into the still with eleven gallons of proof spirit and two gallons of water. As soon as your still begins to work, 'fasten to the nose of your worm two ounces of English saffron tied up in a cloth, that the liquor may run through it and extract all its tincture'. When the operation is finished, you 'dulcify your goods with fine sugar'.

Royal Usquebaugh uses a larger proportion of the above spices and herbs and includes three ounces of ginger and one and a half ounces of mace and cubebs; four and a half ounces of saffron at the worm's end instead of two, and the juice of four and a half pounds of raisins, three pounds of dates and two pounds of liquorice root added after distillation. It would seem that while the English word 'usquebaugh' is definitely from the Gaelic *uisge-beatha*, in its use, it refers to a cordial or liqueur, a spirit, any available spirit in fact, rectified and compounded with herbs and spices.

We have said above that the distilling industry has not been as highly organized commercially in Ireland as in Scotland. But with only three distilleries in the Irish Republic, it was perhaps inevitable that they should merge soon. In fact, the company known as the United Distilleries of Ireland was formed in 1966 with the merger of John Jameson, John Power and the Cork Distilleries Company. In January 1968, its subsidiary, United Distilleries of Ireland (United Kingdom) Ltd. began trading in Britain. The distillers of Ireland have always relied on the home market for the sale of their goods, and at the present time about 75 per cent of their output is consumed on the soil from which it grew. Nevertheless, a strong home market is a favourable enough platform for an export drive, and for the expansion of their overseas markets, it will be interesting to see whether the Irish will rely entirely on the pungent juices of their great pot stills alone, or if they will be enticed to ameliorate them with patent still spirit.

9. The Scots Pint or Tappit Hen

'A Tappit Hen, a bird as peculiar to you as the eagle to Jove, has not been seen among us since that event.' John MacFarlane writing to Duncan Forbes after his return to the North. (see p. 45.)

'Luckie Macleary appeared with a huge pewter pot containing at least three English quarts, familiarily denominated a Tappit Hen, which in the language of the hostess, reamed with excellent claret.' Waverley, Vol. 1.

(From the National Museum of Antiquities of Scotland.)

10.   **Highland bothy – the alarm.** An early posed photograph, but the actors and interior are undoubtedly genuine.

11.   **Poteen making in Connemara.** Children watching the still.

12.   **Whisky on its way in 1924.** The Glenlivet being conveyed by steam
traction to Ballindalloch Station.

(From George & J. G. Smith Ltd, Glenlivet.)

13.   **Irish pot still containing 18,000 gallons.** In Jameson's Bow Street
Distillery the stills range in size between 15,000 gallons and 25,000 gallons.

(From the Irish Whiskey Association.)

14. **Highland pot stills.** 'A multiplicity of small stills'

The still-house at Cardow Distillery, Knockando, Morayshire. When the
distillery was re-built in 1961, although two new stills were added, their
design was based precisely on the old ones. Cardow is a fine malt whisky
and can be obtained fairly easily in bottle on the retail market. Capacity
of stills; Wash 3,650/3,820 galls., Low wines, 3,250 galls.

(*From the library of the Distillers Company Ltd, St James's Square, London.*)

9

Expansion: the 'What is Whisky?' Case

There are two dates in the history of Scotch whisky which are of great significance for the modern industry. The Act of 1823, besides reducing the duty on whisky, allowed it to be warehoused in bond before payment of duty. Thus began the death, albeit slowly, of illicit distilling and the proper beginning of legal distilling. In the phraseology of the times, 'moonlight' was giving way to 'daylight'. The second date is that of the patenting of the Coffey still in 1832. Its speed of action and its great bulk of output were great assets to the distiller. Although one immediate result was a proliferation of would-be 'get rich quick' distillers, this typical invention of the Industrial Revolution was to have a lasting effect on the industry.

For a few decades the ancient craftsmen of pot distilling and the revolutionaries of the patent still remained at peace with one another. The latter consolidated themselves in 1856 when a number of leading distillers in the Lowlands of Scotland entered into a combine to protect their common interests and to prevent over-production. Shortly afterwards the market for whisky began to increase. Boom conditions resulting from the Franco-Prussian war caused a rise in wages in the heavy industries of Scotland and a subsequent increase in drinking. The spread of the vine pest *Phylloxera* through the wine-growing areas of France forced brandy into second place and it has never since recovered. This pest, sometimes called the 'American grape louse', ravaged the vineyards for the last forty years of the nineteenth century.

The overall result of these conditions was that the last decades of the century saw a crazy boom in the whisky industry. The ravages of *Phylloxera* had ousted brandy, and whisky was coming into its own right as a potable self-spirit without further rectification. New companies were formed, new distilleries built and the production of existing ones vastly increased. To exploit this increasing market more fully, a more powerful combine was formed in 1877. The owners of six Lowland distilleries – Cambus, Cameron Bridge, Carsebridge, Glenochil, Kirkliston and Port Dundas – all grain, combined and called themselves the Distillers Company Limited. The nominal capital of the company was £2,000,000, and its registered offices, then as now, were at Torphichen Street, Edinburgh. Although this company is today a household word in blended whisky, it was at that time a grain distillers company only. But the new middlemen, the blenders, were becoming more powerful than ever before and they were afraid that DCL would come to monopolize grain whisky production. In 1885, therefore, a consortium of blenders decided to build their own distillery and they built the North British distillery in Edinburgh. This distillery is still very much in existence and was until a short time ago the most productive plant in Scotland.

By now the finished blend of grain and malt whisky was finding a ready market throughout Britain, but before we look at blending or at the conflict that grew up between the two types of manufacturer in any detail, let us glance at the kind of person who pioneered the sales of Scotch whisky beyond Scotland's borders.

It was not simply the grape louse that advanced the popularity of whisky in England. Very able salesmen went south to advertise their wares. Perhaps the first really successful one was Alexander Walker, son to John Walker, 'born 1820 and still going strong', of Kilmarnock. John Walker was a local licensed grocer, but his son Alexander had been trained in business in Glasgow and he saw the potentialities of the London market for a good blended whisky. By the 1860s he was exporting Scotch to that city in considerable quantities and the year 1880 saw the opening of a London office, followed shortly by a bottling plant. His sons carried on his work, and not being content with being mere blenders of whisky, they became owners of distilleries. They expanded beyond England in the same century and Australia became an important market.

James Buchanan, later Lord Woolavington, was another successful blender and salesman. He began business in London as an employee of a Leith whisky firm but in 1885 he set up his own business. Successful in London, he started an export trade which he supervised personally, to Canada, the United States, South America and New Zealand. In London and the provinces he prospered further. He supplied his 'Royal Household' whisky to the courts of Queen Victoria and Edward VII and he also won a contract to supply the House of Commons with whisky. It was from this contract that the famous Black and White brand name came. The whisky was actually called 'House of Commons' and carried a plain black and white label. Ultimately people simply asked for 'black and white', and that brand name was duly registered.

Some of the household names in the Scotch whisky industry started in a haphazard fashion such as this. William Sanderson, a maker of liqueurs in Leith, decided to enter the blended whisky trade. He made up a hundred different blends and asked his connoisseur friends to help him choose the best one. The one that received the most favourable verdict was numbered 69, hence the famous brand name Vat 69.

The boom continued and many firms who specialized in things other than Scotch whisky were tempted to join the bandwagon. One of the most prominent and successful was the firm of W. & A. Gilbey. With humble resources, the two brothers William and Arthur set themselves up as Cape or South African wine merchants in Oxford Street in 1857. In their stocks they also included 'Universal Brandy'. As they grew they traded increasingly in whisky and they showed a distinct preference for Irish. They were also well ahead in appreciating the attractiveness to the public of a satisfying whisky provided in a bottle. They were quick to see the advance in the popularity of Scotch whisky in England in the eighties, and in 1887 Gilbey's bought the Glen Spey distillery in Scotland.

Less fortunate were the Pattison brothers of Leith. As wholesale grocers in that town, they saw much of the success of the blending trade at first hand and they had heard of the success of the purveyors of blends in markets south of Scotland. In the eighties they moved into the trade in a gimmicky way which was typical of the period. We must remember that at this time advertising by posters tended to be frowned on, and even newspapers had to be discreet with their advertising. Hence some kind of gimmick, or advertising demonstration, was undertaken. Where Buchanan used his black and white horses, the Pattison brothers dispatched hundreds of parrots to licensed grocers throughout Scotland, trained to cry out 'Drink Pattison's whisky'. Their business prospered throughout Britain and they built extensive blending premises in Leith Walk. But their ostentation in advertising their wares and themselves was accompanied by extravagance, and their apparent high plane of success was not to be maintained for long. They fell in December 1898 and their fall caused the whisky boom to collapse. One immediate and important result of the Pattison failure was the entry of the DCL into the blending and wholesale market. They bought their Leith Walk blending plant for £60,000.

The basis of the world-wide success of the modern Scotch whisky industry lay undoubtedly in the success of blending, in a palatable fashion, a number of matured pot still whiskies with a similar quantity, or in many cases, a somewhat larger quantity of matured grain whiskies from patent stills.

Blending seems to have begun first about 1850, and then it was only blending of the same whisky at different ages, all from the same distillery. Attempts were being made, in other words, to make newer whisky more palatable by putting in a dash of older and more mellow spirit. This was a far cry from the sophisticated methods of today when blends can achieve a then undreamt-of individuality of their own. In noting the undoubted success of Scotch whisky around the globe, and the vast amount of revenue it must have gifted to the coffers of many nations, we must bear this fact of blending in mind.

Blending had developed to the extent of mixing pot still with patent still spirits by 1865. This seems to have been pioneered by Andrew Usher & Co of Edinburgh, and although they are now merged in the great Distillers Company group, the whisky that made its name then as Old Vatted Glenlivet can still be had under that label.

There have been many attitudes to blending and its skills. Aeneas MacDonald, in his pungent little book on whisky, says: 'whiskies are capricious, sensitive creatures; they are not to be flung at one another like goats'. Of Lowland malts in a blend he says that their function is 'not to add an instrument to the well balanced orchestra, which every good blend is, but rather to act as the conductor. . . . They act as a bridge between the pungent Highland malts, and the sexless, neutral grain whiskies.' Saintsbury was quite simple in his choice. He preferred a marriage of that richly dour Sutherland whisky, Clynelish, to The Glenlivet. While one suspects that he would rather have had them in separate glasses, Saintsbury was delightfully evading the issue of the growth of the kind of blend on which commercial prosperity was to be based.

That prosperity was not to be achieved easily. The blending of pot and patent still whiskies, or the sale of the 'silent' spirit of the latter, still under the name of whisky, generated an almost ruinous war between the two types of manufacturer. A blast was sounded from across the Irish Sea in the book *Truths about*

Whisky, published in 1878. This was sponsored by four Irish distillers, John Jameson, William Jameson, John Power, and George Roe, in an attempt to check the 'practices of the fraudulent traders by whom silent spirit, variously disguised and flavoured, is sold under the name of Whisky'. True, they had another, and more limited axe to grind, in that they wished to protect the good name of Dublin whisky. At that time, Dublin whisky enjoyed a high reputation in England, so much that unscrupulous traders actually imported cheap spirits from Britain into Dublin so that it could be re-exported again under the label of Dublin whisky. There was, however, widespread agitation about the proper or improper use of the name 'whisky'. All pot still manufacturers would deny the name to patent still spirit, and in Scotland, a number would deny the name even to a pot still spirit, if the barley from which it came were not grown in Scotland.

The Select Committee of 1890–1 concluded that there was no way to define properly spirits going under popular names. They noted that

> There is no exact legal definition of spirits going by popular names, such as whiskey, brandy, rum, patent or silent spirits. Some witnesses desire to define whiskey as the spirit made in pot stills, and would deny that name to spirit made in patent stills, even though the proportion of malt and grain might be the same in both. Some of the distillers from malt desire that their whiskey should be called 'malt whiskey', though the general name whiskey might be extended to those who mix malt with grain.

They also noted other important trends of the times:

> The blending or mixing of different kinds of spirits, chiefly whiskey has now become a large trade. From 13 to 14 million gallons are operated on in warehouses in this way. It is stated that public taste requires whiskey of less

marked characteristics than formerly, and to gratify this desire, various blends are made, either by the mixture of pot still products, or by the addition of silent spirit from the patent stills. In this latter case cheapness is the purpose of the blend, but it is also stated that it incorporates the mixture of several whiskies more efficiently. The blends, even when made from old spirits of various kinds, are frequently kept in bond for a considerable time, although in other cases, they enter into consumption soon after the mixture, according to the requirements or the convenience of the dealers.

In these events and attitudes towards the turn of the present century, we can see a sharpening of the hostility between the pot distillers and the grain distillers and blenders. The failure of the vine and the scarcity of true brandy had led to the appearance of many dubious mixtures that gave the adjective 'blended' a spurious sound. The pot distillers of the Highlands and Ireland felt that their ancient craft was being abused by unscrupulous middlemen and others who still called their product 'whisky'. Furthermore, the success of legal actions against traders in false brandies gave them the resolve to try the issue in court. This decision led to the famous 'What is whisky?' case.

At North London Police Court in November 1905, a Mr. Davidge was charged with a contravention of Section 6 of the Food and Drugs Act of 1875. He was alleged to have sold 'to the prejudice of the purchaser, who demanded Scotch whiskey, something which was not of the nature, substance and quality of Scotch whiskey'. A similar charge was preferred against another shopkeeper, a Mr. Wells, in respect of Irish whiskey.

Dr. Teed, Public Analyst of the Borough of Islington, analysed the samples and certified that each consisted 'entirely of patent still, silent or natural spirits'. His certificate stated that 'whiskey should consist of spirit distilled in a pot still, derived from malted barley, mixed or not with unmalted barley and wheat, or either of them'.

The judgment of the magistrate, Mr. E. Snow Fordham, was a critical one for the industry. He came to the following conclusions.

1 Patent still spirit alone is not whiskey.
2 The product of the patent still unmixed with pot still cannot be Irish or Scotch whiskey although made in Ireland or Scotland.
3 The material to be used to produce Scotch whiskey is wholly barley malt.
4 That maize, not having been used in the pot still or Scotch method of making whiskey, cannot be the material from which whiskey is derived.
5 That what the defendants sold as whiskey was patent still whiskey made largely from maize, to which had been added a dash of less than 10 per cent of Scotch whiskey.

We must acknowledge the sincere belief in their product that the Highland malt distillers possessed. Their skill was the culmination of centuries of carefully nursed tradition, and to them, the product of Aeneas Coffey's invention was trash – a crude and underhand challenge to the heady, flavoursome Highland dew. The 'affair of tall columns', as one writer has described the patent still, was regarded, though as we have already said, not quite correctly, as being neutral and devoid of any flavour.

Yet this was a quarrel among the family. The Distillers Company supported the appeal against Mr. Snow Fordham's judgment that the convicted shopkeepers had sold an article 'not of the nature and substance demanded'. The seven sittings of the appeal court at Clerkenwell were fortunately indecisive, and led ultimately to the setting up of the Royal Commission on Whiskey and other Potable Spirits in 1908. The Commission received its instructions in the following manner:

1 Whether in the general interest of the consumer, or in the interest of public health, or otherwise, it is desirable:
   (a) To place restrictions upon the materials or the processes which may be used in the preparation or manufacture in the United Kingdom, of Scotch Whiskey, Irish Whiskey, or any spirit to which the term Whiskey may be applied as a trade description.
   (b) To require declarations to be made as to the materials, processes of manufacture, or preparation or age, of any such spirit.
   (c) To require a minimum period during which any such spirit should be matured in bond; and
   (d) To extend any requirements of the kind mentioned in the two sub-divisions immediately preceding to any such spirit imported into the United Kingdom.
2 By what means, if it be found desirable that any such restrictions, declarations or period should be prescribed, a uniform practice in this respect may be satisfactorily secured.

Dated 17th February 1908
Signed   H. J. Gladstone

Supported by scientific and medical experts, the Commission respectfully considered whether it was desirable to place such restrictions on materials or methods of manufacture of any spirit to which the name 'whiskey' should be applied, or whether consumer interest or public health was involved in this case. They did much sampling, and they always requested a statement of the age of any spirit that they discussed. This was truly a domestic quarrel and a nasty one. Although it took place after the innovation of blending, the malt party in particular did not seem to realize the great commercial potentiality to themselves in blending malt and grain whiskies. The malt distillers called grain spirit a tasteless distillation that could be made from any rubbish. They also claimed that even if this spirit were blended with malt whisky, it should not be dignified with the name of Scotch whisky. The grain distillers, on the other hand, pointed to the impurities of pot still whisky. Fusel oil, the collective name for higher alcohols, those which have a lower boiling point than the potable ethyl alcohol, was claimed to be injurious to health. While the patent still could draw these higher alcohols off before they entered the final product, the pot still could not. While these contrary arguments raged, however, the fight was for the legal recognition of *blended* whisky.

The Commission made much practical observation and met numerous witnesses, many of whom were biased and some of whom were just ignorant. Dr. Frank Litherland Teed, the Public Analyst for the Borough of Islington, whom we have already met above, did not distinguish himself as a witness, although he claimed to have visited Ireland once and Scotland twice. In his opening evidence, he seemed to rely more on Robert Burns for a definition of whisky than on scientific analysis. He quoted no fewer than fifty-two lines of Burns. He also claimed that Dewars in their whisky exhibition at the Alhambra Music Hall in November 1905 agreed with Burns' notion of what constituted whisky. In this exhibition, Dewars apparently showed fields of barley and pot stills but no maize and no patent still.

Teed was simply using Burns as evidence that whisky was a spirit made from malted barley in a pot still. It was thus all too easy for his interrogator, Dr. Horace T. Brown, to point out that the patent still was not invented until thirty years after Burns's death. Dr. Brown also quoted a pamphlet printed in 1785 on behalf of the Landed Interests of Scotland to the effect that unmalted grain, barley, wheat or rye was used in whisky distilling as well as malted barley. He further quoted the Report of the Select Committee of the House of Commons which sat from 1798 to 1799 to consider the state of the laws relevant to the distillation of spirits in Scotland: 'They use a mixture of malted and unmalted grain, the greater proportion of which is malted.'

To a certain extent the deliberations of the Commission can be seen as a semantic exercise. They clarified somewhat the use of certain terms although perhaps only to the extent of establishing their vagueness. The term 'silent' normally used to denote a patent still spirit is a case in point. The eminent chemist, Dr. Philip Schidrowitz, revealed that it was also used of Lowland malt whisky. He produced in court a sample of a fine Lowland malt, fetching a high price and yet describing itself as a 'silent whisky'. He could only conclude that it was a comparative term, and while the Lowland malt in question was undoubtedly a fine product, it could be regarded as comparatively silent in comparison to, say, an Islay whisky.

Dr. Schidrowitz disagreed with Dr. Teed's conclusion that no genuine pot still whisky contains less than 380 out of 100,000 parts impurities. He believed that it would be impossible to arrive at a controlled chemical definition of whisky, and he would separate chemical analysis from the appreciation of the palate: 'I do not think that the chemical analysis necessarily conforms to the character of the whisky.' As well as being highly skilled in the chemistry of whisky, Schidrowitz also educated his palate. While observing that one can get a variety of readings from the product of a single distillery at different times, he observes also that the whisky maintains its individual character. This is due, he thinks, to the fact that we cannot be sure of the effect that certain constituents, although chemically measurable, can have on the flavour.

A great deal of chemical conjecture appears in the evidence heard before the Commission. For instance, L. N. Guillemard, Deputy Chairman of the Board of Inland Revenue, seriously suggested that chemists alone could run a distillery very effectively. After all, if people objected to a lack of flavour in a patent still spirit through over-rectification, i.e. taking too many of the secondary constituents out of it, the chemists would recover the impurities and dose the finished product with them.

What Saintsbury called 'this most futile commission' issued its final report on 28 July 1909. It recognized that the Select Committee of 1890–1 had already examined most of the questions which were before it, and it gave similar answers. It laid down, let us hope for all time, that:

> Whiskey is a spirit obtained by distillation from a mash of cereal grains, saccharified by the diastase of malt; that Scotch Whiskey is whiskey, as above defined, made in Scotland, and that Irish Whiskey is whiskey, as above defined, made in Ireland.

These findings were described as a triumph for the grain distillers, but today, we can look on it only as a victory for common sense.

In this dispute there was the familiar confrontation of forward-thinking business enterprise and heel-digging tradition. With hindsight we can admire the acumen of the Distillers Company in supporting the appeal of the Islington shopkeepers. It marked the beginning of the unproscribed growth of the industry as we know it today. It also signalled the continued and increasing prosperity of the Highland malt distillers, among them the DCL itself which now owns over forty malt distilleries in Scotland.[1] The findings of the Royal Commission forced an alliance which has made Scotch whisky inimitable, for the basis of the formula which makes all blends Scotch is always the peat-dried malt of the Highland pot stills. This is what has always made imitation a great problem.

While there is imitation in abundance we cannot say that any whisky made outside Scotland or Ireland is necessarily an 'imitation'. For instance we can regard Canadian and American whisky as offshoots of our own. More precisely, Canadian is a cousin twice removed. While distilling from molasses, i.e. rum-making, was known in Canada in the mid-eighteenth century, distilling from grain did not develop until the turn of the nineteenth and this was due to an influx of settlers who arrived after the end of the American Revolution.

In the American Colonies distilling from grain appears to have been carried on in Maryland and Virginia in the seventeenth century. Coming to a later date we know that George Washington sold rye whisky from his own still near Mount Vernon and that he was very proud of its quality. The American whisky industry endured its own peculiar growing pains. In 1791, the Washington administration imposed an Excise tax on the spirit and it was this tax which ultimately sparked off the 'Whisky Insurrection' of 1794. The small farmers were accustomed to convert their surplus grain into whisky and they strongly resisted the tax. Nevertheless, the hated tax gave the industry an impetus. Angry Scottish and Irish settlers moved west beyond the reach of the tax collectors into Indian territory and they found good distilling conditions in Indiana and Kentucky. They also found that the new land was very good for maize growing and this became their chosen grain for distilling. Names such as Spears, Hamilton and Stewart are prominent among the distillers of this period, and as early as 1789 the Reverend Elijah Craig had established a still in Bourbon County. The maize spirit of those areas was much sweeter than the rye spirit of the eastern states and, under the name of 'Bourbon', it became the most popular whisky in America.

When countries such as Holland, Denmark, Japan and Spain make Scotch-type whiskies, that is imitation. These ingenious attempts to copy are in themselves a tribute to the commercial power of the word 'Scotch' in the world today. I have only tried a few of them but some come nearer bourbon in character than they do Scotch. I am sorry I missed the bizarre experience of a friend of mine who was offered a whisky with the name 'King Edward the First' while visiting Vienna.

I understand that there is a whisky on the market in Japan with the name 'King Anne'. Some of the Scotch-type whiskies that one meets on the Continent defy analysis by the palate in terms of a comparison with any known Scotch whisky. This is not to say that they are all simply bad. Indeed, I have tried a Dutch one which was quite palatable and probably the most pleasing of the imitations that I have tried but at the same time it bore no relation to Scotch. The most atrocious fluid that I have seen masquerading under the name Scotch was in Denmark. Yet there seems to be little that can be done as long as the copyright of a registered name is not contravened. When that is so, legal action can be taken, as in the case in the twenties when the proprietors of White Horse whisky brought a successful action against a German firm marketing a German spirit called 'Black and White Horse Whisky'.

To speak in this manner is not to decry the drinks of other nations. It is to condemn the attempted short cut to commercial success at the expense of those who first pioneered the way. Other nations have their drinks of national fame. No one could complain of the rums, vodkas, schnapps and other drinks that have an honourable place in the traditions of those who make them, and are indeed palatable to many others.

Blending got a great boost after the 'What is whisky?' case and its aftermath, and now it is a highly specialized job. Behind the great labels are formulas which are followed with a definite quality and character as a goal. The blender must not only be able to recognize and judge a large number of whiskies, but he must also be able to assess the capabilities of single malt whiskies of mingling satisfactorily with specific grain whiskies. He must also be able to judge the character of malt and grain whiskies in their new state. I remember being in the office of the chairman, and chief blender, of a great whisky company.[2] On a table before him were new whiskies from the forty or so distilleries which his firm dealt with for mature whiskies for their blends. He told me that he was 'keeping an eye on this week's distillation'. The judgment of the skilled blender is not based physically on his palate, because, if he did base his assessment of every whisky on actually tasting it, his palate would be ruined. Only very occasionally does he take a sip, and then only if he suspects that there is some quality in it that has escaped the nose. He uses various ways of stimulating the bouquet which is his guide to quality and character. First of all the over-proof spirit straight from the still or the bond must be 'awakened' by the addition of water, and put in the nosing glass, a tall tulip-shaped glass which narrows towards the top and concentrates the bouquet. When the whisky is cold its flavour is suppressed, and the hand must supply stimulating heat through the delicate glass. Some blenders rub a small amount on the palms of their hands, cup their palms and nose it in that manner.

The mature whiskies are blended at over-proof strength and thoroughly mixed in vats, either by wooden stirrers, or as is more usual today, by compressed air. They are then stored for some time together, and this stage of the process is called 'marrying'. Some firms 'vat' their whiskies, that is, they blend their malt and grain whiskies separately and bring them together only just before bottling. At this stage, before bottling, the whisky has to be broken down to 30 under-proof, or whatever other strength may be required for any particular market. At this stage the whisky has to be very finely filtered. This is because some of the secondary constituents of the spirit are less soluble at the lower alcoholic strength and they form themselves into minute solids, making the liquid cloudy. Although this cloudiness is quite harmless, it is the practice to remove it.

The water needed to bring the whisky down to the required under-proof strength must be soft and many blenders have to go to some expense and trouble to obtain it. Some blenders, however, are very fortunate through their geographical location. In the city of Glasgow, for instance, the public supply of water is very soft and contains only a very minute quantity of solid matter.

While most of the well-known blends in this country are available at 70 proof, single malt whiskies are to be had at strengths of 80 and 100 and even beyond. Also some of the big blending companies have what they call a de-luxe or five-star blend. These normally have a greater proportion of mature single whiskies in them and cost a couple of shillings more. For instance, Haig's have 'Dimple', Crawford's have 'Five-star', Mackinlay's have 'Legacy', and so on.

The normal strength of blended whisky at consumer level in the United Kingdom was not always 70 proof. Before the First World War the strength was customarily 80 proof. In one of those fits of inexplicable behaviour that seems endemic in British Governments, the outfit of that period decided to enforce the lowering of spirit strength to 70 proof before the public should be allowed to consume it. True to character they back-pedalled and in 1921 they decided to permit the sale of whisky at the old strength of 80 proof. By this time they had contrived to raise the tax on it at the new weaker strength and the traders were naturally loath to raise the price still further by going back to the old strength. They pointed out that the first step towards reverting to the old strength was for the Government to reduce taxation.

Saintsbury had his own comment on this legislation, saying that 'the abominable tyranny of the enforced breaking down to thirty under proof has spoilt the ethers of the older whiskies terribly'. Of course, Saintsbury had his own distinctive views on the treatment of whisky. For instance, he agreed with a number of connoisseurs of his day that whisky kept in the same cask for over fifteen years tended to become slimy. To avoid this he suggested doing what all persons of 'some sense and some means north of the Tweed formerly did, establishing a cask'. To do this you take any cask from a butt (110 gallons), an octave (14 gallons), or an anker (10 gallons) or even less, fill it up with a good drinkable whisky, stand it on end and fix a tap halfway down. When the level of the whisky reaches the tap, top the cask up with a drinkable but not too new whisky. You are thus establishing a *solera*, after the manner of sherry. The new whisky is suitably doctored by the older contents of the cask, and these are refreshed by the new. Saintsbury himself practised this method in octave casks, and supplied his vessels with Clynelish, The Glenlivet, Glen Grant, Talisker, and one Islay brand. He was also partial to the single malt Long John, from the complex now known as the Ben Nevis distillery, and to Glendronach. He furthermore allowed himself the luxury of keeping independent jars of these whiskies.

One of the notable features of twentieth-century industry and commerce has been the formation of combines and vast mergers. Scotch whisky has been no exception. We have already noticed that in 1877 six grain distilleries banded themselves together into a powerful combination to be known as the Distillers Company Limited. When the Caledonian grain distillery joined the group in 1884, the blenders regarded the DCL as having a virtual monopoly of grain distilling. Resenting such a control over a vital constituent of their finished product, the blenders decided to build a grain distillery of their own, and in the following year they built the 'independent' North British distillery in Edinburgh. Moves of this kind tended to inspire counter-moves, and this particular move by a strong consortium of blenders drove DCL out of its position as a grain whisky combine into acquiring malt distilleries and ultimately into the blending trade itself.

Despite the genius of merchants such as Walker, Buchanan, Dewar and Sanderson, the end of the road was in sight for the individual trader. In the light of further acquisitions by DCL in the first decade or so of this century, the firms of Buchanan and Dewar amalgamated and forged ahead to become, by the early twenties, the largest whisky enterprise in Britain, the second largest being the Distillers Company.

It may seem strange to the layman that when the two giants ultimately amalgamated in 1925, the larger company took the name of the lesser, DCL. In simple terms, the explanation is that the DCL offered to more than double its existing authorized capital to provide for future extensions to the combine, and the larger company, Buchanan-Dewar, agreed. This remarkable feat of the takeover of a larger company by a lesser was primarily due to the skill of the then managing director of DCL, William H. Ross. In the same year, the third largest company and great competitor, Johnny Walker, joined the group to make DCL one of the largest industrial enterprises in Great Britain. Two years later White Horse joined. William Sanderson's of Vat 69 came in in 1937, bringing with them not only their own considerable whisky interests but also the London gin firm of Booth's. The DCL had already acquired Gordon's Gin (1922) when the company bought the Distillers Finance Corporation. This Corporation controlled Gordon's and a number of distilling and other concerns in Scotland and Ireland. Ironically enough, Booth's at the time reacted strongly to the DCL intrusion into the London gin trade, and to strengthen their own position, had bought Wandsworth distillery. This is now a highly modernized DCL grain distillery.

It would be superfluous here to try to delineate the numerous activities of DCL. In the year after its inception it had already shown its teeth outside Scotland by buying the Phoenix Park distillery in Dublin. With the acquisition of the Caledonian distillery in the eighties came a breakthrough into the gin rectifying business in London, through interests owned by the proprietors of Caledonian in Tooley Street.

Perhaps it should be emphasized that a *rectifying* distillery for the production of gin requires a distilled grain spirit for its raw material. This was a problem for DCL at the time. It had either to buy the grain spirit for Tooley Street from rival grain distillers in England or else transport it from

Scotland. By 1910 DCL had solved the problem in character-
istic fashion. It bought Hammersmith distillery, one of the
three distilleries then in existence in London.

In acquiring the Vauxhall distillery of Liverpool in 1907
they had strengthened their hold of the English market in
methylated spirits and industrial spirits. In these moves the
DCL was freeing its Scottish distilleries from the burden of
supporting the company's interests outside the whisky trade.
This was at a time when Scotch whisky was enjoying a boom
and very little grain spirit could be spared for other purposes.
The company's chemical interests are now legion.

It has been said that the appetite of the DCL grew with
eating. In the years between the wars particularly, amalgamation was preached and practised. Sometimes the practice
of amalgamation involved the purchasing of a distillery or other
plant and then closing it down. This invoked frowns and
mutterings of monopoly, but in many cases the acquired
distillery would have gone bankrupt anyway and the owner
was glad to sell it.

It is important to emphasize that the DCL, although a
vast company in the whisky industry and outside it, and
owning over forty malt distilleries and five grain distilleries in
Scotland, is by no means synonymous with the whisky trade.
Over and above the great companies financed by capital from
overseas, such as Hiram Walker and Schenley, there are
'little men' who have grown big while retaining their family
identity. Typical of these is the firm of William Grant of
'Stand Fast'.

The founder of the firm which bears his name was born in
humble circumstances in 1839 and spent the beginning of his
working life as an apprentice shoe-maker. He later became manager of the Kininver lime works with the hope of setting up a
lime works himself. To our good fortune he abandoned this idea
and entered Mortlach distillery as a clerk in 1860. He was at
that distillery for twenty years until, with his son John, he

bought a piece of land by the Fiddich burn. There, William Grant and his son simply began to build a distillery with their own hands. With a little money provided by his own modest savings, and assistance from his two eldest sons, one a lawyer and the other a schoolmaster, he bought the second-hand equipment of the old Cardow distillery for £120. The Glenfiddich distillery was completed in a little over a year and the first whisky was run on Christmas Day 1887. The malt in the kiln was dried by peat cut by William Grant's daughters.

No doubt assisted by the boom conditions of the time, William Grant was able to build another distillery, Balvenie, also on the Fiddich burn, within a period of five years. Both distilleries were renovated in 1955, and Glenfiddich, with its twelve pot stills, is one of the largest in the Highlands. In 1962 the firm built a giant grain distillery at Girvan in Ayrshire. The plant incorporates a Lowland malt distillery and a rectifying unit for gin. The Lowland malt is called Ladyburn. The time taken to build the grain distillery was quite a record. Instead of the estimated two years, it was completed in nine months. The famous 'Stand Fast' is the main blend of the firm but the ten-year-old Glenfiddich is readily available out of the same triangular bottle at 70 proof. I have heard that Balvenie is also available at the hair-raising strength of 106·4 proof but I have not tried it.

One of the most elusive of the imponderables of malt whiskies is the individual character of each. This capacity for individuality is at its most remarkable when two distilleries are in close proximity and their common factors can be isolated. Glenfiddich and Balvenie are a case in point. Grant's manager at Girvan, Mr. MacNaughton, previously at the Highland distilleries, described the common factors which prevailed at the two – the same malt, the same yeast, the same water supply and the same management. The only known different element is the size of the stills where Glenfiddich's twelve stills, seven spirit and five wash, are half the size of Balvenie's six. Yet the overall situation is that Balvenie is 'cut' at 15 over-proof and Glenfiddich at 10 in order to achieve the best results. In maturation, again, Balvenie reaches its peak in about ten years while the ideal age for Glenfiddich is reckoned to be twelve years.

The popular blend 'Bells' of Arthur Bell & Son of Perth also began in a humble fashion. But the story of Bells is not one of a distiller enlarging his operations towards blending and distribution. Bells, or what was to become Bells, began in a small whisky shop which was opened in Perth in 1825 by T. R. Sandeman. In 1851 he was joined by Arthur Bell who ultimately took control of the firm. Until the end of the century, the firm remained essentially small blenders with none of their own distilleries to fall back on for supplies. They showed remarkable courage in the slump conditions of the thirties when they bought the Highland malt distilleries of Blair Atholl, Dufftown, and Inchgower at Buckie. All three distilleries have been modernized, with Blair Atholl being a bit of a showpiece, and blending and bottling plants are established in Perth and Edinburgh. While the main final product of the company is the popular blend 'Bells', both Blair Atholl and Dufftown are bottled as single whiskies at 80 proof and are much sought after.

Notes to chapter.

[1] Thirty-nine operative at present.
[2] Hiram Walker, Ltd., Dumbarton.

10

The Industry of Today

The history of Scotch whisky between the wars follows closely to the economic pattern in the country. Initially, just after the First World War, distilling resumed in a burst of false confidence, and in a year or two declined into a phase of depression. The home market suffered in succession from Austen Chamberlain's raising of the excise duty to give the public the famous 12s. 6d. per bottle, the general strike of 1926, the shock wave of the Wall Street collapse of 1929 and the following depression of the early years of the thirties.

Prohibition in the United States helped Scotch in an important way. Through it, Scotch whisky gained a position of prestige in the United States which it has never relinquished. It has been remarked that Prohibition did not stop the liquor traffic, it merely changed it. While America's legal imports dropped to a minute quantity, those of her neighbours multiplied. Perhaps an extreme example is the Bahamas. In 1918, they took 944 gallons of Scotch and in 1921 they took 386,000. In the years from 1918 to 1920 (Prohibition began on 19 January 1920) Canada's imports increased from 149,000 proof gallons to 1,702,000. One small island convenient to the American coast actually imported just under twenty proof gallons of Scotch per head of the population.

The reason why these phenomenal rises took place is not difficult to see. The thirst of the 'dry' American nation was vast and it preferred the bootlegged Scotch to the native moonshine. Its more adventurous citizens manned armadas of small craft and plied their trade with the many neighbours who stockpiled so generously for them. The American Government complained to Britain about the volume of bootlegging trade being carried on from West Indian ports, but as British law was not being violated, nothing significant could be done. So with the ease with which the unpopular ban could be violated, and since all distilling for the public had been banned in America, Scotch increased its business greatly and gained a hold on the American palate which has increased ever since. Despite the ban, which was enforced on the coastline by hundreds of small armed vessels and seaplanes, a wide selection of the best Scotch whiskies got through to the American cities. The 'noble experiment' was doomed to failure. The repeal of Prohibition was one of the main issues on which Franklin D. Roosevelt fought his first successful campaign for the Presidency of the United States. The Repeal was announced on 5 December 1933.

Following the end of Prohibition and the recommencement of liquor imports, some difficulty was encountered by the agents of Scotch in the idea that each country importing to the United States should be restricted to a prearranged quota. This was dropped, however, and Scotch whisky gained free access to its greatest market. There was a little further trouble in the definition of whisky. The Americans had not had their equivalent of our 'What is whisky?' case, nor of our Royal Commission of 1909 which followed it, and they had their own views of what constituted whisky. This question also came to be settled amicably.

There is still some ill-feeling, particularly in the Bourbon Institute, about the quantity of Scotch whisky that is being imported into the United States. These are the words of J. F. O'Connell, President of the US Association of Alcoholic Beverage Importers, in reply to these sentiments.

The makers of Scotch whisky have marketed their product throughout the world in fair weather and foul. Their experience in merchandising is enormous and their reputation for product consistency and availability is an invaluable asset. Contrast these circumstances with the handicap of the producer of American spirits. He represents an industry recalled to life in 1933 after having been killed and interred thirteen years earlier by the catastrophe called National Prohibition.

(*Wine and Spirit Trade Record*, October 1966)

Today, we tend to associate the American market with the 'light' whisky fad. This adjective is a little puzzling and seems to carry with it something of the connotation of 'neutral'. Certainly, a number of those blends which go out of their way to advertise themselves as 'light' do not seem to have any easily discernible malt content. The Americans are bigger consumers of mixed drinks than most people and it may be that our exporters wish to supply them with something less pungent in flavour than Bourbon or rye for the purposes of mixing. The extreme in light whisky would seem to be the product being marketed at the present time by McGuinness Distillers of Canada. It is described by the company as 'the world's first aged rye whisky'. From reports, it is made by filtering mature whisky to remove the flavour and odour and then reflavouring it very slightly with a trace of the ordinary mature spirit.

Light whisky is now being made in the United States itself. The American Distilling Company of Illinois is at present manufacturing large quantities of this kind of spirit to be matured in used barrels. This is a new departure in American spirit legislation, since their distillers have never been allowed to use barrels more than once. This is not only a burden of extra expense on the distiller but is also a barrier to the production of a light whisky since new barrels tend to give a woody flavour to a distillation.

The changes in the law will not apply to Bourbon or rye whisky. The official reasons given were that to mature Bourbon or rye in used casks would destroy their distinctiveness. While the brewing processes and the distillation method by themselves were not distinctive, should the maturation method be changed, the names of these whiskies would be meaningless. Incidentally, this change in the American law may be an added burden to the distiller of Scotch whisky. While the ideal vessel for maturing Scotch whisky is a used sherry cask, the next best is a used Bourbon or rye cask. They will still be on the market but their availability for the Scotch trade will depend on the extent of the requirements of the distillers of the new 'light whisky'.

Another facet of the industry between the wars and during the last three decades or so has been the appearance of foreign interests on the local scene. Undoubtedly the biggest of these is the Canadian firm of Hiram Walker. Distillers in Ontario since 1858, they entered the Scotch trade in 1930 with the purchase of a majority share in two blending companies. In 1936 they acquired Ballantine's, which remains their chief blended whisky, and the malt distilleries of Glen Burgie and Milton Duff. In order to balance their production potential, they built their own grain distillery at Dumbarton. This plant was completed in 1938. At the present time, the distilling and blending complex at Dumbarton presents an impressive sight. Covering seventy-five acres, it not only embraces their giant grain still but also their Lowland malt still, Inverleven, all blending and bottling facilities for their 'Ballantine's', 'Ambassador' and 'Old Smuggler' and many acres of bonded warehouses.

The Future

A great deal has been written about the future of Scotch whisky. It is difficult for anyone either outside or inside the trade to make any more than a guess as to the continuity

147

of the high wave of commercial success on which it is riding at the present time. But it is possible for the many reputable people in the trade and the *cognoscenti* among the drinking public to agree on one thing, and that is, a fundamental factor in the continuity of prosperity has by and large already been achieved. There are a large number of blends of a high quality readily available on the retail markets at home and abroad, and in recent years the number of well-matured malts from individual distilleries has increased to the extent that it is possible for the discerning drinker to see clearly the regional patterns of character and flavour that we hear about so often, and also to see the subtle variations of flavour within those regions. Quality of the high standard already existing must be maintained as an essential ingredient in any future success. This factor, together with the expertise to develop and hold markets, is within the grasp of the industry and is an established part of the blueprint for the future.

It is difficult to say, as one looking in from outside, whether the industry itself is capable of curbing the danger of over-production, should that danger arise. Our benevolent Jeremiah from the north, Mr. Birnie of Glen Mhor, is by no means new in his pessimism. What could be stronger than the warnings of the DCL about the 'serious menace' of over-production in the years immediately after the First World War? These were warnings backed by action. Distilleries were acquired and promptly closed, and the company closed some of its own. But this concern about over-production in those years arose presumably from a reading of the economic situation of the country – from a vision of shrinking markets due to diminishing buying capacity. To this may be added the rising taxation on whisky with which we are becoming only too familiar.

It is undoubtedly this factor of penal taxation coupled with uncertainty about the economic state of our nation that led DCL to run down its malt whisky production during 1968. Initially, the plans announced involved the maltings only of some twenty-six distilleries and four independent maltings. The broad reason given was 'reduced demand for new malt whisky'. The actual distillery floor maltings selected for closure were 'old and uneconomic to operate'. It was disturbing to find later in the year that three of the distilleries listed as losing their maltings were to close completely. These include Oban and Glengarioch, two of the oldest distilleries in Scotland. Oban was established in 1794 by the MacLeans of Lochbuy in Mull. Glengarioch is at Old Meldrum in Aberdeenshire, and the entry for the parish in *The Older Statistical Account* records that there is 'a brewery and distillery lately established'. It was an old Sanderson property. The third one is Glenlochy, near Fort William, built in 1878, and passing under DCL control as late as 1953.

It is depressing to hear of closures of such distilleries, particularly when Scotch whisky exports appear to be leaping forward. Apart from the obvious one of the marked decline in home consumption, another cause for apprehension on the part of producers may be the rise in the production of 'light whisky' in the United States. This has been estimated at 160 million gallons by 1972. Producers of this type of spirit are confident that they can cut in on the sales of Scotch. It is the aim of the American distillers to produce a whisky that will have a taste comparable to Scotch, while at the same time avoiding any reference to this attempted copying in their brand names. In this way they hope to avoid the odium which became attached to their 'Scotch-type Whisky', now extinct. This was a blend between an American neutral spirit and imported Scotch malt whisky. Their Internal Revenue Service defines 'light whisky' as a whisky which has been 'distilled in the US at more than 160 proof (142·5 British), stored in used or new uncharred oak containers, and bottled at not less than 80 proof (70 British). It can be called "blended light whisky" if mixed with not more than 20 per cent of other straight whisky'.

In their attempts to produce a cheaper product, the Americans will certainly be helped by the permission to use the cheaper used barrels, but it is doubtful if they can imitate Scotch simply by the reuse of maturing containers. The conditions for maturing pertaining in Scotland and America are vastly different. The cool temperature and the humidity in the bonded warehouses in Scotland must be very different from these factors in their American counterparts, leading to marked differences in the final product.

Despite these developments across the seas, Scotch whisky exports showed a remarkable increase in 1968. The increase was most marked in America where their imports of Scotch showed an increase in one month, August, of 220 per cent. This very unusual increase pointed to stockpiling by importers against the threat of a longshoremen's strike in the autumn. But the exports to other countries are substantially up also. France, the second biggest overseas market, showed an increase of nearly half a million gallons. Exports to West Germany, Belgium, Australia, Italy, Brazil and Japan also showed substantial increases. Canada, a difficult market in which some well-known exporters report a decline, nevertheless showed an important overall increase.

But the whisky producer is never without his problems and forebodings. We can imagine Scotch whisky producers, and assiduous drinkers, waking up some nights with a nasty dream, the subject of that dream being the six nations of the Common Market of Europe. If Britain joined the Common Market it would be an economic event that would make forecasts based on statistics look rather pointless. The only certain statement that we can make about this eventuality is that should it take place, things will not be as they are. As is well known, the Scotch whisky industry is dependent for manufacturing supplies to a great extent on countries outwith the Common Market. As none of the Six can supply any substantial quantities of grains suitable for distilling, the tariffs against these imports by Britain would undoubtedly increase the cost of production. On the subject of the harmonizing of internal duties, the *Wine and Spirit Trade Record* is delightfully and subtly optimistic. I would like to quote from their issue of August 1967.

> The *Record* is of the opinion that one reason behind the present fantastic and unreal rate of spirit duties in the United Kingdom is to allow a bargaining point in Common Market negotiations: the Chancellor and the British 'negotiators', will unwillingly 'consent' to a reduction in internal spirit duties in the interests of the Six, and try to get a more valuable concession for themselves as a *quid pro quo.*

We can only hope that our successive Chancellors of the Exchequer are as cunning and assiduous in the interests of the public as the *Record* would have them be.

Perhaps it is not fully realized how long Scotch whisky has kept its price stable. Its actual cost to the consumer is at the whim of any Chancellor who cannot balance his books, but the actual price of it has not gone up one penny since 1961. Higher costs for materials, wages and other things have been absorbed without passing any part of these on to the consumer. The last increase was an increase to the public of 1s. 6d. per bottle; of this threepence went to the producer. The residue, 1s. 3d., was divided between the wholesaler and the retailer.

In basic terms, you may pay a price of 52s. for a good and accredited blend of Scotch whisky. As you do so, please remember that you are paying 6s. for the actual commodity and 46s. to your government. If you translate this ratio into a transaction for the purchase of a car or a television set, the fact of this penal taxation will strike you hard.

Further Reading

BARNARD, A., *The Whisky Distilleries of the United Kingdom*, London, 1887; re-printed, 1969.

GILLESPIE, Malcolm, *Memorial and Case of Malcolm Gillespie, Officer of Excise, Skene, Aberdeenshire*, Aberdeen, 1826.

GLENLIVET, *The Annals of the Distillery*, 1924 and 1959.

LOCKHART, R. Bruce, *Scotch*, London, 1959.

MACDONALD, Aeneas, *Whisky*, Edinburgh, 1930.

MACDONALD, Ian, *Smuggling in the Highlands*, Inverness, 1914.

SILLETT, S. T., *Illicit Scotch*, Aberdeen, 1965.

TATE, F. G. H., *Alcoholometry*, HMSO, 1930.

WILSON, ROSS, *Scotch Made Easy*, London, 1959. This writer has contributed three series of important articles to the *Wine and Spirit Trade Record* in recent years. 'Scotch Whisky Distillers of Today', 'Seventy Years of the Scotch Whisky Industry', and 'Pioneers of the Scotch Whisky Industry'.

Whisky: Thoughts on distillation of ardent spirits in the Highlands of Scotland; submitted to the consideration of the government by a landed proprietor in the county of Inverness, Inverness, 1814.

Index

(The phrase 'malt distillery' without further definition refers to Highland malt.)

Achanalt, 86
Act of
 1579, controlling distilling, 3
 1644, first Act of Excise, 6
 1729, first anti-gin Act, 17–18
 1733, anti-gin, 18
 1736, anti-gin, 18–19; repealed, 19
 1784, anent Ferintosh, quoted, 68–9
 1784, Wash Act, 68, 71
 1786, Distillery Licence Act, 66, 70
 1787, defining Lowland and Highland boundaries, quoted, 68
 1787, Hydrometer Act, 96
 1798, 69
 1814, 70–1
 1818, Hydrometer Act, 98
 1823, 88, 91, 123
Ailligin, 87
Ale, 38–9; two-penny, 48–9, 61, 63
Ambassador blend, 147
American distilling, 135
Aqua vitae, 2–5
Ardmore malt distillery, 111
Arnott, Hugo, quoted, 61–2
Arthur, George, Supervisor of Excise, 78
Auchentoshan Lowland malt distillery, 110–11

Baleshare, *see* MacDonald
Ballantine's blend, 147
Balvenie malt distillery, 142—3
Banff, 39
Barber Surgeons, ix, 3—4, 15–16

Barbet still, 112
Bell, Arthur & Son, 143
Bicker, *see* Drinking Vessels
Birnie, William, C. A., 148
Black and White blend, 125
Black and White Horse, 136
Blagden, Sir Charles, 96–7
Blair Atholl malt distillery, 143
Blending, 100, 124–9, 136–8
Boisdale, *see* Macdonald
Bonnie-wife's tavern, 39
Boswell, Sir Alexander, caption facing p. 27
Bourbon, 135, 145–7
Brandy, English, 17; French, 16, 123–4; Glasgow, 121; Parliament, 18; Spanish, 31; Universal, 126; uncustomed, 60
Bribes, 76
Bridekirk, Lady, 46, 57
Brown, Dr. Horace T., 137
Bryden, 32
Buchanan, James, 125, 129
Burke, Edward, 51
Burns, Robert, 15, 55, 69, 132; quoted, 29–31; as Exciseman, 32
Burt, Edward, quoted, 40–2, 44–5
Burton, Hill, quoted, 42–3
Bushell, Captain, 9–11

Cademan, Dr. Thomas, 16
Campbell, Rev. Archibald, 36
Campbeltown, 110
Cardow malt distillery, 142
Carlyle, Alexander, quoted, 46–7, 57
Carr, Sir John, quoted, 48
Chambers, Robert, 49

Change-house, 63
Charles 11, 16
Charlie, Bonnie Prince, 49–55
Chemists, 114–15
Chisolm, Rev., quoted, 36–7
Cholera, epidemic of 1832, 5
Chopin, *see* Drinking Vessels
Clanranald, Macdonalds of, 23–4, 27
Claret, 4–5, 8, 38, 45, 47, 56
Clarke, John, his Hydrometer and
    Brandy Prover, 95–8
Clergy and drinking, 36–8
Clonmacnoise, Annals of, 2
Clynelish malt, 127, 129
Cobbett, M. P., quoted, 48
Coffey, Aeneas, and his patent still,
    112, 123
Committee of Enquiry (1802), 97
Cooper, A., 1, 121
Cor, Friar John, 2
Coridale, Glen, 50

Damien, John, Abbot of Tungland,
    alchemist, 2
Deanston malt distillery, 104, 107,
    118
Dearg, John, 81–2
Defoe, Daniel, quoted, 17, 121
Dewars, 132, 139
Distillers Company Limited, 124,
    126–7, 130, 134, 139–41, 148–9
Drink in Scotland in 18th century,
    4–5
Drinking Vessels, 55–6
Dublin whisky, 128
Dufftown malt distillery, 143

Edinburgh City Fathers, 14
Edradour malt distillery, 103, 105,
    107, 111
English Worshipful Company of
    Distillers, 16

Ferintosh, 58–9, 61, 68–9
Forbes, Arthur, 68–9
Forbes, Bumper John, 44–5
Forbes, Duncan, Lord President, 4,
    43, quoted, 45–6, 60; 'chartered
    boast', 58; relevant Act quoted,
    58–9

Forbes, Sir William of Pitsligo, 69
Fraser, Simon Lord Lovat, 4–5,
    41–3
Funerals in the Highlands, 64–5

Geneva, 15, 17, 28–9, 36
Gentleman's Magazine, quoted, 17
Gilbey, W. A., 125–6
Gillespie, Malcolm, 75–8
Gin, 15, 17; gin age, 17–20; bogus
    names, 19; Booth's, Gordon's, 140
Glendronach malt whisky, 139
Glenfiddich malt distillery, 142–3
Glengarioch malt distillery, 149
Glenlivet, The, 88–93, 109, 111, 127
Glenlivet, Old Vatted, 127
Glenmorangie malt distillery, 107
Grain whisky, 112–14, 127, 127–30,
    132–3, 140–1
Grant, Mrs., of Laggan, quoted,
    47–8
Grant, William, 141–2

Haig, John and James, 69
Hammersmith grain distillery, 141
Healey, Maurice, 116
Hiram Walker, 136, 141, 147
Home, Rev. George, quoted, 63

Inchgower malt distillery, 143
Inverleven Lowland malt distillery,
    147
Iona, Statutes of, quoted, 24, 26
Irish whiskey, 116–22
Islay, Earl of, quoted, 19
Isle of Jura malt distillery, 107

Jacobite National Anthem, quoted,
    53
James IV, King of Scots, 2
Jameson, John, 118, 120, 122

Kintail, 36
Kirk, Thomas, quoted, 38, 39

Ladyburn Lowland malt distillery,
    103, 142
Laphroaig Islay malt distillery, 111
Lecky, W. E. H., quoted, 17
Leyden, Dr. John, quoted, 72–3

Licence system, 66–7
Light whisky, 146–7
Lindsay, William, 37
Littlemill Lowland malt distillery, 104
Loch Lomond malt distillery, 104–105, 107
Loch nan Uamh, 49, 52
Long John, 119, 139
Lowland malt, see Auchentoshan, Inverleven, Kinclaith, Ladyburn
Lully, Raymond, alchemist, 1

Macallan-Glenlivet, 109, 111
Mac an Aba, Fransai Mor, J. P., 75
MacDonald, Aeneas, quoted, 127
MacDonald, Alasdair, quoted, 28
MacDonald, Flora, 51–2
MacDonald, Ian, 69, 81; quoted, 83–5
MacDonald of Baleshare, 50
MacDonald of Boisdale, 50
MacDonald of Kingsburgh, 51, 52
Macintosh of Borlum, quoted, 5
MacIntyre, Duncan Ban, 28
MacKenzie, Osgood, quoted, 80
MacKinnon, Nan, quoted, 35–6
MacLeod, Donald, of Galtrigill, 50, 52
MacLeod, Rory Mor of Dunvegan, 22, and caption facing p. 26
MacNaughton, distillery manager, 142
MacNeil, 27
MacPherson, Lachlan of Strathmasie, quoted, 33–4
MacPherson, Robbie, 83
MacVurich, quoted, 33–4
Magranell, Richard, 2
Malt Tax riots, 7–12, 58
McGuinness Distillers of Canada, 146
Middlesex petition on gin drinking, quoted, 18
Miller, Provost, 9–11
Mitchell, Bailie, 11
Morison, Fynes, 3
Munro, Capt. H., quoted, 74–5
Murray, C. de B., quoted, 8
Mutchkin, see Drinking vessels

North British grain distillery, 124, 139

Oban malt distillery, 149
O'Connell, F. J., quoted, 145–6
Old Smuggler blended whisky, 147

Patent still, see Aenas Coffey and Grain whisky
Pattison brothers, 126
Piracy of wine ships in the Minch, 27
Phoenix Park Irish distillery, 140
Phylloxera, 123–4
Pope, Alexander, quoted, 18
Porteous Riot, 12–15
Power, John, 122
Prohibition, 144–5
Proof defined, 95–5
Punch, 5, 39, 51

Raasay, Island of, 51
Ramsay, Allen, quoted, 13
Ramsay, John of Ochtertyre, quoted 56
Roup and conviviality, 47
Roxburghe, Duke of, 12
Royal Commission of 1908–1909, 130–34
Ross, William H., 140

Saintsbury, 127, 134, 138–9
Sandeman, T. R., 143
Sanderson, William, 125, 129
Salt, contraband, 49
Scott, Sir Walter, 72, 89
Select Committee of 1890–1891, quoted, 128–9
Schenley, 141
Schidrowitz, Dr. Philip, 133
Shawfield, Daniel Campbell of, 9, 12
Sikes, Bartholomew, 97–9
Silent spirit, see Grain whisky
Sillett, S. W., 76
Smith, D. H., 121
Smith, George, 90–2
Smollett, Tobias, quoted, 63–5
Smuggling, see Chapters 4 & 5
Southey, Robert, Poet Laureate, quoted, 48–9

Spenser, Edmund, quoted, 25
Stark, John, Dean of Guild, 11
Statistical Account, quoted, 73
Stein, James and John, 69
Stein, Robert, 112
Steuart, James, 54
Stewart, Col. of Garth, quoted, 71–2, 74, 79
Sylvius, Professor of Leyden, 15

Talisker malt whisky, 110–11
Tappit Hen, 45–65
Tea, 5, 61–3; smuggled, 61
Teed, Dr. F. L., 129, 132–3
Telford, 48–9
Thoresby, Ralph, F. R. S., 39
Toypnett, see Drinking vessels.
Truths about whisky, quoted, 128
Tytler, William, 54

United Distilleries of Ireland, 122
Usher, Andrew, 127

Usquebaugh, 39, 121–2

Vat 69, 125
Vauxhall grain distillery, 141

Wade, General, 10
Walker, Alexander and John, 124–125, 139
Walpole, Prime Minister, quoted, 12
Wandsworth grain distillery, 140
Warner, Robert, total abstainer, 6
Washington, George, 135
Webster, Dr. Alexander, 37–8, 45
West Highland malt, compared with Highland, 110
Whisky and Whiskey, terms defined, 116
Whisky Insurrection, 1794, 135
White Horse, 136, 140
Wig Club, 49
William, Dutch, 16, 30
Wilson, Ross, quoted, 67, 110